FIND YOUR SOULMATE NOW

9 Steps That Will Guide You to the Love of Your Life

Jeanne Severe

T0384481

10-10-10
Publishing

FIND YOUR SOULMATE NOW:
9 Steps That Will Give You to the Love of Your Life
www.Search4Soulmate.com
Copyright © 2022 Jeanne Severe

ISBN 979-8-35099-107-9

References to internet websites (URLs) were accurate at the time of writing. Authors and the publishers are not responsible for URLs that may have expired or changed since the manuscript was prepared.

Limits of Liability and Disclaimer of Warranty
The author and publisher shall not be liable for your misuse of the enclosed material. This book is strictly for informational and educational purposes only.

Warning – Disclaimer
The purpose of this book is to educate and entertain. The author and/or publisher do not guarantee that anyone following these techniques, suggestions, tips, ideas, or strategies will become successful. The author and/or publisher shall have neither liability nor responsibility to anyone with respect to any loss or damage caused, or alleged to be caused, directly or indirectly by the information contained in this book.

Publisher
10-10-10 Publishing
Markham, ON   Canada

Printed in Canada and the United States of America

To my daughter and family:
Ericka, my daughter
Jason, my grandson
Samuel, my brother
Marleine, my niece
Marie Geralde, my niece

Table of Contents

About the Author

I, Jeanne Severe, am a physician assistant in internal medicine, and I live in Queens, NY. At age 13, my parents sent me to Bible school in my country. I graduated with a pastorate degree at age 16. I spent the next 30 years as a singer, worshiping God with the choir in NYC. I was married. I have a beautiful daughter and a grandson. I wrote a book by myself before 2021, but then I realized that there were lots of things I needed to know if I wanted to continue to write books.

I saw an ad on the internet about the Raymond Aaron program, which teaches the basics of writing a book. I signed up right away. I attended two days of the boot camp, online in December 2021. Mr. Aaron is a brilliant teacher! This boot camp revolutionized my life. I followed his instructions to write my book, *Find Your Soulmate Now*. I finished writing this book in 30 days. This book will teach you step by step how to embark on the great adventure to find your soulmate, the love of your life!

The author is available for delivering keynote presentations to appropriate audiences. For rates and availability, please contact the author directly at joy.severe@gmail.com.

Finally, if you have been inspired by this book, the best thing you could ever do is to pass it on and be a wonderful role model for others. This world needs more shining lights.

Acknowledgments

I give thanks to God, my creator, who sent his son Jesus Christ to die on the cross and save me from my sins. It is through Him that I have salvation and the guarantee of an eternity in Heaven. He has shown me that He is with me always, and that I should live my life to bless others.

To my daughter Ericka, who has given me the encouragement and has held me accountable to complete *Find Your Soulmate*. You have been my most profound cheering section. None of my accomplishments would have been possible without your constant support.

A special thanks to my grandson Jason, who is the joy of my life. He gives me the courage to write this book.

I would like to thank Raymond Aaron for his excellent 10/10/10 program, which encouraged me to write this book. Because of his dedication and commitment to help others achieve their goals, I was able to finish writing my book, *Find Your Soulmate*, in 30 days. This book will teach about the ten steps to find your soulmate.

I would like to thank Lee Arnold, the founder and CEO of Cogo Capital, who is my mentor and has taught me the basics of real estate investment.

Thank you to Ron Le Gran, a genius in real estate investment, who has transformed my life with his teaching on foreclosure properties.

I appreciate everything that I learned from Scott Carson, who taught me the principles of "notes investment."

I am extremely grateful to Joshua Rosenthal, MS Ed, founder and CEO of IIN School of Nutrition, for teaching me the principles of nutrition, and helping me earn my health coach certificate in nutrition.

Thank you to Dr. Neal Bernard, an excellent teacher at the IIN school of nutrition.

I appreciate Dr. Mark Hyman, an excellent teacher at the IIN school of nutrition.

A special thanks to Pastor Jack Hibbs for teaching me to walk according to God's will for my life.

A special thanks to my pastor, Tim Delina, the pastor of Times Square Church, New York City, who encourages me to walk with God every day of my life.

Foreword

Would you like to find your soulmate?

A simple question, perhaps, but looking for a soulmate can be quite intimidating. It can be like looking for a needle in a haystack ... a daunting task sometimes.

Find Your Soulmate will teach you the nine steps you need to follow, as you embark on the greatest adventure of your life. Be prepared to smile. As Mother Teresa said, "Let us always meet each other with a smile, for the smile is the beginning of love."

This book will encourage you to challenge your beliefs, find your values, and learn to be yourself. By being truthful to yourself and others, you can find not only love, but also a sense of personal power.

In this book, you will:

- explore the interlinking cycle of beliefs, values, actions and outcomes, each of which reinforces the others
- hone your skill at becoming an authentic person, true to your beliefs and values
- start to become more powerful, and understand how that power feeds and supports your beliefs

For bonuses go to www.Search4Soulmate.com

If you are interested in learning how to succeed or build an achievable relationship, then you have found the right book! Rise up; you are on the stage, and the world is yours. This is your moment to shine.

Falling in love is an amazing feeling. *Find Your Soulmate* will start you on your journey toward the perfect relationship for you!

Raymond Aaron
New York Times **Bestselling Author**

Chapter 1

Are You Looking for Your Soulmate?

Seeking a soulmate is a major task and a universal necessity for a man or a woman to look into. When the time comes in their life, or they reach a certain age, they start looking for a personal person they can trust; a person who is honest, caring, educated, kind and loving, and a person who is trustworthy and, of course, who has a job and has some money in the bank. This book will show you the way to build a lasting relationship.

Definition of a Soulmate

The Oxford dictionary defines a soulmate as a person ideally suited to another as a close friend or romantic partner. When you find someone who shares the same values and desires as you in life, and it is someone who is patient, respects your space and complements you, then that person can become your soulmate. Look out for that person, and take time to know each other. This book will help you find your soulmate. The Earth is full to capacity with men and women; however, it's very difficult for a man or a woman to discover each other and build a stable relationship and complement each other. This book will show you the way to build a lasting relationship.

Here we are talking about generosity. The first quality to seek in a soulmate is generosity. Your soulmate should be generous toward you. He should offer unconditional help in time of need. Your true spiritual soulmate is the person who is intended to help you complete yourself. Believe it or not, there is somebody out there for you. That person will fall in love with you regardless of your flaws.

Psalms 24:7-10 (NIV) reads: Lift up your heads, O ye gates, and be lifted up you ancient doors that the King of glory may come in. Who is this King of glory? The Lord strong and mighty, the Lord mighty in battle. Lift up your heads, O ye gates lift them up you ancient doors that the King of glory may come in. Who is this King of glory? The Lord strong and mighty. Has your head been hanging low? Whatever it is that keeps your head low, today is the day to make a change; there is hope in your situation. Things that keep your head hanging low, keep you functioning at a low altitude. The dictionary defines hanging your head as: "to express shame, contrition or embarrassment; to appear embarrassed or ashamed." You have no strength to "take the bull by the horns and deal with it." That means that if the problems that you are facing in life have crushed your spirit, and when you let it happen, you remain hopeless and helpless. You, me—all of us—can do better than that.

David, the author of Psalms 24:1, reads: "The Earth is the Lord's, and all its fullness, the world and those who dwell therein." If the Earth belongs to God and the fullness thereof—the trees, the firmament, the oceans, the sun, the moon, the earth and stars, the universe, the people—then everything belongs to God, and all that live here on Earth and in the heavens belong to God. That's how it will remain until

4

eternity. God has absolute authority over everything on the Earth, in the sky and everything that moves under the oceans. You need to live a happy life because God is working on that soulmate that you are looking for. He will bring him to you as a finished product, complete and lacking nothing.

Trust God. He is going to satisfy the desire of your heart. This is what God does best. He created the person. He created you and knows exactly what you will be. He created you, knowing that you will have a desire to love and to be loved. He knows the pain that you are going through right now—the anguish of the sleepless nights because of the loneliness that you are experiencing right now—but He is working behind the scenes to bring the right person into your life to make you complete. You wonder if there is a person for you out there, and how you can find him/her. Surely, God has a good match for you. You need to be specific in your prayers to God, in order to help you find your soulmate. Humble yourself before the Lord; ask him to intervene, and be specific in requesting what you want, because God said in his word, "If you ask anything in my name, I will do it." You ask God through prayer. Ask God to forgive your sins. Surrender your life to him; then pray to receive your soulmate. Continue to pray, and keep asking him; you will receive the soulmate that God has for you.

"If you ask for bread, God is not going to give you a rock."

The Bible tells us in Luke 11:9-11: "And I say unto you, 'Ask, and it shall be given you; seek, and ye shall find; knock, and it shall be opened unto you. For every one that asketh, receiveth; and he that seeketh, findeth; and to him that knocketh, it shall be opened. If a son shall ask bread of any of you that is a father, will he give him a stone? Or if he asks for a fish, will he give him a serpent?'"

God is your father, and He provides food for you every day. You are able to get up in the morning and go to work and make the money to buy the food that you need to nourish your body every day. God provides you with the job and gives you the strength to do so. You need to have a relationship with God, by repenting of your sins and accepting him as your savior. Now when you pray to him, He will help you.

God Knows What is Best for You

Whether you believe him or not, He's in the process of making and shaping that person for you. If you fast and pray, and seek help from God, He will definitely know who that person is, and you will definitely meet that person someday; but in the meantime, you need to work on yourself. You know what your weaknesses are. You need to be able to have the heart of a servant to be able to serve others.

Meeting somebody can be done through an act of kindness, such as simply opening the door for someone who is walking behind you, until that person completely gets through the door, or by helping to carry a bag of groceries up a flight of stairs for an elderly person. Your act of kindness will pay off someday, because an elderly person has children, nephews and nieces, and you never know who they know. Just be kind always, and you will receive a reward someday for your good deeds.

Juliette's Act of Kindness Brings About the Soulmate That Marries Her

I know a young lady called Juliette. She has the true characteristics of a soulmate. She was kind; she showed empathy and was ready to help. I have known Juliette for several years. She has never had a bad day. She is always kind, jovial, easy going and is always smiling at everybody, and she's always ready to offer help to anyone for anything they need. It was summertime in New York city, and the temperature was about 90 degrees on a Sunday afternoon after church. A group of young adults decided to take a walk in Central Park. In the group was a doctor. He was wearing a suit, a long-sleeved shirt and a tie because he had attended the church service in the morning. He was joining the group for a walk in Central Park in the afternoon. The people in the group wore comfortable, casual clothes like T-shirts, sneakers and short pants, to make it easier to really enjoy their walking adventure in the park. As the group was walking along in the park, Juliette observed that the doctor was overdressed for the occasion, and that he looked uncomfortable and was sweating like crazy. Juliette gently approached him and kindly said, "Hi, my name is Juliette. It's very hot today, and I am sure you are sweating. If you take off your jacket, I will carry it for you."

The doctor was overjoyed and amazed by the kindness that Juliette showed toward him. A friendship started the same day, followed by a relationship. Juliette and the doctor got engaged within three months. After one year, they were happily married, and they lived happily ever after. You never know when or where your soulmate is going to show up. Be vigilant and be nice always! You never know when you are going to meet that special person who could very well become your soulmate. Keep your eyes open, keep your ears open and keep your mind open to people that you are passing by every day, and to people that you are meeting every day. Pay attention to the needs of others because you never know when it's going to be the day that you meet that special person who could become the love of your life, your soulmate.

The Discovery Phase and Dating

Dating is a discovery period. It is a fact-finding phase where you get involved with someone, you go in with a reasonable level of trust and then use your discoveries like an internal system of checks and balances.

During the discovery phase, it's time to find out who that person is. What is he or she looking for in this relationship? It's time to learn about each other, good or bad experiences all included. Ask that question: Do you want to be in a relationship with me but are afraid of commitment? Let him or her know that you are serious about finding a relationship that will last. Ask him or her: Are you afraid to be alone? Some people cannot live alone; they just need somebody to pass the time. What they do is to spend some time with you for a few months, and then they tell you some excuses and disappear.

During discovery, it's like going to an interview with both eyes and ears open; assess what you see and hear. You need clarity of mind to make the right decision. If you are looking for a soulmate, look no further; the answer is in this book. Evaluate your inner self: How do you feel? What makes you happy or sad? What do you need to do to put yourself on the right track to find your soulmate? Take time for yourself, and meditate on things that you will step out to do that will bring success to your life. Work on your flaws; nobody is perfect. We mess up things every day, and we fix things every day, either in our actions or attitudes toward others, and all that happens in our minds. "It was found that the average person has about 6,000 thoughts going through their mind in a single day."

https://www.newshub.co.nz/home/lifestyle/2020/07/new-study-reveals-just-how-many-thoughts-we-have-each-day.html

I wonder how many of these thoughts are used in a positive way to bless somebody and to send good wishes toward someone you love. Use those positive thoughts to personally pray to God for yourself. Let your request be known to God, and He will give you the desire of your heart. Just ask your Father, have faith, believe that you will receive it and it shall come to pass.

Do Due Diligence to Screen Your Soulmate

When you do due diligence, you want to find out who you are dealing with. Sincerely, you will. You had better do due diligence, because you are ready to venture out into unknown territory. You feel vulnerable not knowing who is sitting across the table in the restaurant or the coffee shop. It's good to meet in a place where there are other people in the room. A soulmate is someone who comes into your life to teach, push and transcend you into a higher state of consciousness and being. These are the questions to ask:

1. Have you been married before?
2. Do you want to have children?
3. If the person says no, and you know you want to have children, end the conversation; you decide.

If he says yes, you can ask more questions about children and see where that leads.

Are you close with your family?

Do a self-inventory on how you feel about him, in the first few days after you meet him.

Three months and six months later, reassess your feelings toward your relationship.

During the romance phase, don't get blinded by passion; you need more than love to move to the next phase.

Let's speak about some practical guidelines to follow when you want to get married. Don't marry a man who has no job. The Bible tells us that "those that do not work should not eat." Be wise in your decision-making plan, and always make the right choice. Don't marry outside the church. Don't become unequally yoked with unbelievers. No room for divorce God said in his words, what God put together no man put asunder. Don't fall for a smooth-talking man with a deep voice, who calls you in the middle of the night to tell you, "I think you are the angel that I saw in my dream last night," or "Hey, I want to wake up next to you every morning, my sweetheart; can you make it happen?" You are their shining light. Remember one thing: "Men are by nature hunters, and women have been put in the position of being the prey," as quoted by Steve Harvey. Let's review this: Men are hunters; women are the prey. Be wise; don't fall into their traps. Use those tips to protect yourself. Ask your soulmate this question: "Do you know the Ten Commandments and which ones you cannot keep?" It's good to know about the Ten Commandments. I am going to list them here for you:

The Ten Commandments

And God spoke all these words:

"I am the LORD your God, who brought you out of Egypt, out of the land of slavery. You shall have no other gods before me. You shall not make for yourself an image in the form of anything in heaven above or on the earth beneath or in the waters below. You shall not bow down to them or worship them; for I, the LORD your God, am a jealous God, punishing the children for the sin of the parents to the third and fourth generation of those who hate me, but showing love to a thousand generations of those who love me and keep my commandments. You shall not misuse the name of the LORD your God, for the LORD will not hold anyone guiltless who misuses his name.

"Remember the Sabbath day by keeping it holy. Six days, you shall labor and do all your work, but the seventh day is a Sabbath to the LORD your God. On it, you shall not do any work, neither you, nor your son or daughter, nor your male or female servant, nor your animals, nor any foreigner residing in your towns.
https://www.biblegateway.com/passage/
?search=Exodus%2020&version=NIV.

God spoke the Ten Commandments, and the words were being written on two tablets of stone, which were given to Moses for the Israelites to follow the writing instructions. The first four commandments told us to worship only God and not to serve idols. The purpose of the 10 commandments is to show us what God wants us to do, to find faith in him and to serve him.

Don't marry a girl who cannot cook. It is a good thing when a woman can prepare a few dishes to surprise their soulmate. These days, there are succulent meals already prepared in the frozen food section of the supermarket; you just have to follow directions. Use a microwave or oven to cook for 20–30 minutes or heat and serve. Let's talk a little bit about marriage. Marriage is a choice; you make your own decision. The decision to get married to your soulmate comes from your brain. Wow! The specialized nerve cells in your brain communicate with each other to help you make the right decision of whom to marry. It's your responsibility to choose the right person to marry.

Don't rush into anything. Your gut feeling is also involved. Your friends, family members, your mother and your father, your grandmother and grandfather, your priest or your pastor can give you advice about the choice that you made. Check also with a marriage counselor, which can help you sort out things that you haven't even perceived that could happen down the line. Speak with a pastor. Because of his experience with his church members and God's guidance, he would tell you exactly what he perceives could happen down the road, which you won't be able to actually detect in your own understanding. Besides that, the pastor is anointed by God to discern if the outcome is going to be beneficial to you. Look for God's wisdom to help you discern the right move to make. Seek God's help, and pray. When you pray, you can think more clearly.

The Bible tells us in Proverbs 3:5-7 NIV: "Trust in the Lord with all thine heart; and lean not unto thine own understanding. In all thy ways acknowledge him, and He shall direct thy paths. Be not wise in thine own eyes; fear the Lord, and depart from evil." Seek guidance from your parents, and do not venture out without their input in the decision making, because they have been there and done that. They are able to lead you in the right direction. The Bible tells us: "Children, **obey your parents in the Lord**, for this is right. "That it may go well with you and that you may enjoy long life on the earth." Ephesians 6:1 (NIV) Young ladies and young men, you need your parents' blessings in the decisions that you make in life, to prevent you from getting into a potential nightmare.

For bonuses go to ...

How to Detect Red Flags in a Relationship

A red flag is essentially a signal that goes off when something's not right, intuitively telling you to steer clear. In the case of relationships, they'll show up when the object of your affection does or says something that rubs you the wrong way and makes you question the relationship. Sometimes these red flags can be less extreme, and other times they're a crystal clear sign to run for the hills. According to psychotherapist and relationship expert Ken Page, LSCW: "They can range from "proceed with caution," to "absolutely don't go there," depending on the severity of the behavior and your own relationship patterns."
https://www.mindbodygreen.com/articles/red-flags-in-relationships

"If they say, for instance, that they will never get married, and that's something you desire, then believe them."
– Dr. Wendy Walsh

Replace bad habits with positive ones.

1. **Buying things that you don't need.** I have a friend who is an example of having an emotional roller coaster spending attitude. In the past ten years, she has had the tendency to go on a spending spree. If she gets upset about something that has not gone as expected, she says to herself: "I am going to get even; I am going shopping." She will go to an expensive boutique, and she will buy six to eight pairs of shoes in one day. Then she will go

to a "chic boutique," where the rich and famous buy their clothes, and she will buy about six to ten dresses, maxing out her credit card and taking a taxi home to carry all her stuff. When she arrives at the building where she lives, there are usually two to three neighbors who would say, "Here comes Miss Fashion; let's go and help her out. They would go to the taxi and help Miss Fashion empty out the taxi. Later on that day, she would call me on the phone and say, "I took vengeance over not having my way from whatever the situation was, but I beat it, and I feel great about myself. YES, I did it!" She felt empowered, she felt great and her anger went away. The euphoria of having new clothes and new shoes appeased her anger for the moment, but the bills were going to catch up with her. She thought she was a winner until the bills arrived in the mail the following month. Then she realized and thought, "Oh, my gosh! What have I done? I was so stupid; that was not the right thing to do. I have become a slave of the creditors. Some of these clothes, I will never wear. Now I have to take control over spending, what I buy and when I buy it. One thing I have found is that the clothes that I am buying are good quality, but I am on a yoyo diet, and my weight goes up and down, so some of the clothes I bought are already too small for me. I will ditch that roller coaster emotional spending and take control over my financial freedom."

2. **Picking your nose.** (That's gross, especially in front of people— yikes!) That's the norm for some people, don't get me wrong. It's much better to clean up your nose when you are taking a shower and nobody is watching you. However, if you have a cold and you need to blow your nose, go to the corner and do it, or into the

bathroom where nobody is watching you. Wash your hands with soap, and then go back to the dinner table or to your computer, and continue to do what you're doing. Enough of that; this is not a pleasant topic to speak about.

3. **Biting your fingernails.** What causes people generally to bite their nails? Nail biting is closely related to anxiety. Nervous people chew their nails, and it causes pain, discomfort and bleeding, until infection occurs. For any infected nail, visit your medical doctor. He or she will tell you exactly what to do. People that bite their nails feel a sensation of pleasure and relief. Those people feel ashamed about the nail biting, because they can damage the tissue around the fingers, the mouth and their teeth. So it's not a good thing for people to constantly chew their nails. The chewing nails phenomena starts during childhood. Children that have been neglected display emotional behavior, and they develop the bad habit of chewing their nails. If you're a nail-biting adult, chances are good that you picked up the habit when you were young. But there are good reasons to break the habit. (Quote source Maria A. Scremin DO https://www.cedars-sinai.org/blog/stop-nail-biting.html)

4. **Eating fast food.** Fast food does not contain the proper nutrients that your body needs. It is high in sugar, salt and saturated or trans fats. Having junk food regularly is bad for you. It has been shown to lead to **increased risks of obesity and chronic diseases.** Cardiovascular disease, type 2 diabetes, non-alcoholic fatty liver disease and some cancers all have been caused by excessive junk

food consumption. Make a change in your diet today. Your energy level will increase, and your body will thank you.

5. Spending less than 20 seconds washing your hands. Washing your hands is very important in order to kill germs that we encounter everywhere. Your hands touch everything and carry germs from different sources. So it's good to wash your hands to get rid of the germs, which if ingested could make you sick.

Learn a new language.

Knowing how to speak more than one language opens the door for you to meet more people. Polish your original language. In whatever language you speak, increase your vocabulary. Learn songs in that language. Listen to classical, jazz and country music, and music that has repetitive words and compels you to sing along. By learning a new language, you can translate English into French or Spanish, and vice versa, which can make you more desirable in your job. You are always going to find clients that do not speak English and need translation. You will be the right person to go to for translation. When you go to a party, and if you understand that people in your close environment speak a language and can understand, you will be the one to translate the conversation, which opens up your circle of "polyglot" friends. Learn some romantic songs in French. You may be able to impress somebody someday; you never know. For example:

1. Hymne a L'amour, by Edith Piaf
2. Only You, by The Platters

3. My Heart Will Go On, by Celine Dion
4. Les Plus Belles Chansons, by Charles Aznavour, and many more.

Learn a few sentences in French, and go to a 5-star French restaurant for your birthday. Tell the chef in French that today is your birthday, and enjoy a delicious meal!

Work on yourself to become a better you. Exercise, read books, take new courses and learn to cook new dishes. Learn to bake a cake or cookies. Enjoy your life. Love and spend time with your family and friends.

Chapter 2

Characteristics of Your Soulmate

Your Soulmate Is Ready to Compromise

When you create your work schedule, you set aside time for you and your soulmate to spend together, like planning a family vacation together or going to dinner together. Have a barbecue with the family together. Play ping pong or volleyball, or go bicycle riding with your family and friends. Worship together and pray together, and tell funny jokes and laugh together. Review a spending plan, and balance a budget together.

Your Soulmate and You Need to Sit Down and Start a Conversation

Your soulmate and you need to sit down and start a conversation. Your soulmate should be able to approach any issue with an open mind. Listen to what is being said by the other party, without interruption. Be fair, and put yourself in your soulmate's shoes; feel what he or she feels, and be ready to put some options on the table so that the two of you can pick and choose from them. Pick an option and stick with it. Be ready to forgive each other, shake it off and let it go.

For bonuses go to ...

Your Soulmate Is Trustworthy

Your soulmate should be trustworthy. You should feel safe when you are around him. Create an image in your mind that you are able to attract a trustworthy person into your life. Trust and believe in yourself, and you will see it happen. Love yourself. Take good care of yourself.

Your Soulmate Should Support Your Passions and Decisions

Your soulmate should support your passions and decisions. A soulmate always brings a smile to your face. It's the person you think about when you first wake up in the morning, and it's the last person you think about before you fall asleep at night. That soulmate is always on your mind, day and night.

Your Soulmate Is Humorous

Your real soulmate has a great sense of humor. One soulmate could be chopping up fresh vegetables, and seasoning the steak, and the other one could be setting the table. With the music in the background, they keep talking and laughing, and within a few minutes, the dinner is ready. Laughter is very important in a relationship. Be playful and bring out of him that little boy he used to be, or that little girl.

Your Soulmate Is Loving and Caring

A soulmate is there for you, checking out when you go to work, and making sure everything is all right. You can get a text or email telling you how much he or she misses you and can't wait to see you at home tonight, to try the new Italian dish that he or she prepared specially for you. You will be pleasantly surprised when you get home.

Chapter 3

The Great Adventure to Find the Love That You Deserve

3

When you are looking for a soulmate, you feel like you are embarking on a great adventure to find the love that you deserve. What interests you in your soulmate? You may be looking for a soulmate that is nice, gentle, caring, loving, tall, generous, handsome and compassionate, and with a good sense of humor. That person must have a job, have cash in the bank, life insurance, etc.

What Actions Are You Taking to Lead You to Your Soulmate?

Are you trusting the Lord to help you find this person? Genesis 2:18 (NKJV) says: "And the Lord God said, 'It is not good that man should be alone; I will make him a helper comparable to him.'" Are you looking high and low to find that person? The Bible says: "Lift up your head O ye gates, and be ye lift up ye everlasting doors; and the King of glory shall come in." Who is this King of glory? The Lord strong and mighty, the Lord mighty in battle. Ecclesiastes 3:14-15 says: "I know that whatsoever God doeth, it shall be forever; nothing can be put to it, nor any thing taken from it, and God doeth it, that men should fear before him. That which hath been is now, and that which is to be hath already been; and God requireth that which is past."

Keep Your Head High, Smile and Remain Positive

The sovereignty of God works in your romantic life. Talking about the sovereignty of God denotes that God is in complete control of the Universe. I believe in God; He is not so distant in your life and in your decisions that you are making every day. He gave you free will, so make the right choice that does not have negative consequences. Whatever God determines to do in your life, He has the ability to accomplish it, because his promises are yes and amen. If you are part of the family of God, you can claim this promise in Romans 8:28 (NIV): "And we know that in all things God works for the good of those who love him, who have been called according to his purpose." This verse reassures us that God is working with two things that qualify any circumstance in our life, to work together for our good and for those who love God and are called according to his purpose. The Bible tells us in Proverbs 18:22: "He who finds a wife finds a good thing and receives favor from the Lord." God wants to favor you with a good wife; God wants to bless you with the woman that was created just for you. Be confident and start looking, because God wants to fulfill the desire of your heart.

Use Wisdom and Understanding to Look for Your Soulmate

Those whom he foreknew, he predestined in the book of Ephesians 1:3-14 (NIV):

"Praise be to the God and Father of our Lord Jesus Christ, who has blessed us in the heavenly realms with every spiritual blessing in

Christ. For He chose us in him before the creation of the world to be holy and blameless in his sight. In love, He predestined us for adoption to sonship through Jesus Christ, in accordance with his pleasure and will to the praise of his glorious grace, which he has freely given us in the One he loves. In him we have redemption through his blood, the forgiveness of sins, in accordance with the riches of God's grace that He lavished on us. With all wisdom and understanding, He made known to us the mystery of his will according to his good pleasure, which He purposed in Christ, to be put into effect when the times reach their fulfillment, to bring unity to all things in heaven and on earth under Christ. In him, we were also chosen, having been predestined according to the plan of him who works out everything in conformity with the purpose of his will, in order that we, who were the first to put our hope in Christ, might be for the praise of his glory. And you also were included in Christ when you heard the message of truth, the gospel of your salvation. When you believed, you were marked in him with a seal, the promised Holy Spirit, who is a deposit guaranteeing our inheritance until the redemption of those who are God's possession, to the praise of his glory."

You Are Called to a Glorious Destiny

For those Jesus called his own, He has appointed us to the most glorious of all destinies, to be conformed to the image of his Son so that this time could be. Therefore, we know that God will work all things for our good, because He not only chooses for himself and conditionally, but He has also appointed our destiny. The sovereignty of God impacts everyday life. Jesus came to save us. We accept our salvation by faith in Christ alone. We trust him and follow his commandments. God, right now, is sitting at the right hand of his Father and praying for you and for me. You are wonderfully and beautifully made in the likeness of God. He loves you, and He is working behind the scenes to fulfill the desire of your heart. God did not spare his own son but gave him up for us to show how He will graciously give us all things that pertain to his will. Nobody can bring any charge against those whom God has chosen; it is God who is justified! God knows all things. He created you and me and put love in our hearts. Think for a moment that He is going to satisfy that love with what He knows best. He created the person that will make you complete. Be confident; God will send you the perfect match to make you complete. Ask God, your provider, to send a good match for you.

Have Faith in God; the Answer Is in This Book

God wants to be part of every aspect of your, life including who you marry. The Bible is the way God communicates with you. You need to seek guidance from the Lord for situations that arise in your life. You need to prayerfully open the Bible and ask God to direct you to the verse that speaks directly to your problem. Then you follow the leading of the Holy Spirit for what to do. Continue to pray until you find direct revelation from God to bring about your soulmate.

In the Bible, let's read Proverbs 30:10-31: "Who can find a virtuous woman? For her price is far above rubies. The heart of her husband doth safely trust in her, so that he shall have no need of spoil. She will do him good and not evil all the days of her life. She seeketh wool and flax, and worketh willingly with her hands. She is like the merchants' ships; she bringeth her food from afar. Riseth also while it is yet night, and giveth meat to her household, and a portion to her maidens. She considereth a field, and buyeth it; with the fruit of her hands she planteth a vineyard. She sets about her work vigorously; her arms are strong for her tasks. She sees that her trading is profitable, and her lamp does not go out at night. In her hand, she holds the distaff and grasps the spindle with her fingers. She opens her arms to the poor and extends her hands to the needy. When it snows, she has no fear for her household, for all of them are clothed in scarlet. She makes coverings for her bed; she is clothed in fine linen and purple. Her husband is respected at the city gate, where he takes his seat among the elders of the land. She makes linen garments and sells them, and supplies the merchants with sashes. She is clothed with strength and dignity; she can laugh at the days to come. She speaks with wisdom, and faithful instruction is on her tongue. She watches over the affairs of her household and does not eat the bread of idleness. Her children arise and call her blessed; her husband also, and he praises her: 'Many women do noble things, but you surpass them all.'"

Charm is deceptive, and beauty is fleeting; but a woman who fears the LORD is to be praised. Honor her for all that her hands have done, and let her works bring her praise at the city gate. The virtuous do lots of things; what a great example for us women to follow. She does good to her man all the days of her life. She is multitalented. She wears several hats. She brings food from afar. She makes beautiful clothes for her children. She works at home. She considers a vineyard and buys it with money she makes. She has strong hands and vigorously works with her hands. Her husband is well respected in the city. She does some trading investment; her lamp stays on late at night. The list goes on and on. There are many times that mothers are torn with the worry of their children or family. Even when everyone is sleeping, she is up worrying about her children, often bearing the load of the family. Sometimes we wonder how we will make it, but the strength of a virtuous woman is not depending on herself or her own strength but on the strength of Jesus. She is invested with a moral force and dignity that arms her against cares and worry. Her strength is not in what a man can offer her, not in what she can get from a man, and not in her beauty or money. Her strength lies in her clothed armor of the Lord.

She sets aside time for prayer for herself and for her children. She trusts in the Lord at all times and continually sings praises to the Lord. She is committed to follow the Lord and his leading in her life. Often, we sing that song, "Wherever He leads me, I will follow." She always prays and believes tomorrow will be a better day, and for her heart's desire to come to pass. Whenever the bills are due, just trust in the Lord. In sickness, just trust in the Lord. Where can you find a virtuous woman? You can find her praying in the morning, noonday and evening. You can find her praising God at home, in the community, at work, in church and among friends. You can find a virtuous woman visiting someone in the hospital, helping the poor and needy in the street. You can find a virtuous woman sharing the love of God in her community. A virtuous woman loves God with all her strength, mind and soul. A virtuous woman loves her neighbor as herself.

This is the Story of Samson. Samson was a judge that God appointed over Israel. Samson was called by the Lord to help free the Israelites from the Philistines, their enemy. Samson's mission would require physical strength. The Lord made a covenant with Samson that as long as he obeyed the Lord, he would be physically strong. You will become pregnant and have a son whose head is never to be touched by a razor, because the boy is to be a Nazirite, dedicated to God from the womb. He will take the lead in delivering Israel from the hands of the Philistines (see Judges 13:5 NIV). Samson's long hair was a sign of this covenant. Even though his family had taken a Nazarite vow, he did not follow the guidelines by any stretch. He wreaked havoc and revenge on the Philistines in often violent ways, but worst of all...he fell for Delilah.

"Then went Samson to Gaza, and saw there a harlot, and went in unto her. And it was told the Gazaites, saying, Samson is come hither. And they compassed him in, and laid wait for him all night in the gate of the city, and were quiet all the night, saying, in the morning, when it is day, we shall kill him. And Samson lay till midnight, and arose at midnight, and took the doors of the gate of the city, and the two posts, and went away with them, bar and all, and put them upon his shoulders and carried them up to the top of a hill that is before Hebron.

"And it came to pass afterward that he loved a woman in the valley of Sorek, whose name was Delilah. And the lords of the Philistines came up unto her and said unto her, 'Entice him, and see wherein his great strength lieth and by what means we may prevail against him, that we may bind him to afflict him; and we will give thee every one of us eleven hundred pieces of silver.' And Delilah said to Samson, 'Tell me, I pray thee, wherein thy great strength lieth, and wherewith thou mightest be bound to afflict thee?' And Samson said unto her, 'If they bind me with seven green withs that were never dried, then shall I be weak and be as another man.' Then the lords of the Philistines brought up to her seven green withs, which had not been dried, and she bound him with them. Now there were men lying in wait, abiding with her in the chamber. And she said unto him, 'The Philistines be upon thee, Samson.' And he brake the withs, as a thread of tow is broken when it toucheth the fire. So his strength was not known. And Delilah said unto Samson, 'Behold, thou hast mocked and told me lies; now tell me, I pray thee, wherewith thou mightest be bound?' And he said unto her, 'If they bind me fast with new ropes that never were occupied, then shall I be weak, and be as another man.' Delilah therefore took new ropes, and bound him therewith, and said unto him, 'The Philistines be upon thee, Samson.' And there were liers in wait abiding in the chamber. And he brake them from off his arms like a thread.

"And Delilah said unto Samson, 'Hitherto thou hast mocked me, and told me lies; tell me wherewith thou mightest be bound.' And he said unto her, 'If thou weavest the seven locks of my head with the web.' And she fastened it with the pin, and said unto him, 'The Philistines be upon thee, Samson.' And he awaked out of his sleep, and went away with the pin of the beam, and with the web. And she said unto him, 'How canst thou say, I love thee, when thine heart is not with me? Thou hast mocked me these three times, and hast not told me wherein thy great strength lieth.'

"And it came to pass, when she pressed him daily with her words, and urged him, so that his soul was vexed unto death; that he told her all his heart, and said unto her, 'There hath not come a razor upon mine head; for I have been a Nazarite unto God from my mother's womb: if I be shaven, then my strength will go from me, and I shall become weak, and be like any other man.' And when Delilah saw that he had told her all his heart, she sent and called for the lords of the Philistines, saying, 'Come up this once, for he hath shewed me all his heart.' Then the lords of the Philistines came up unto her, and brought money in their hand. And she made him sleep upon her knees; and she called for a man, and she caused him to shave off the seven locks of his head; and she began to afflict him, and his strength went from him. And she said, 'The Philistines be upon thee, Samson.'

"And he awoke out of his sleep, and said, 'I will go out as at other times before, and shake myself.' And he wist not that the LORD was departed from him. But the Philistines took him, and put out his eyes, and brought him down to Gaza, and bound him with fetters of brass; and he did grind in the prison house. Howbeit the hair of his head began to grow again after he was shaven. Then the lords of the Philistines gathered them together for to offer a great sacrifice unto Dagon their god, and to rejoice: for they said, 'Our god hath delivered Samson our enemy into our hand.' And when the people saw him, they praised their god: for they said, 'Our god hath delivered into our hands our enemy, and the destroyer of our country, which slew many of us.'

"And it came to pass, when their hearts were merry, that they said, 'Call for Samson, that he may make us sport.' And they called for Samson out of the prison house; and he made them sport: and they set him between the pillars. And Samson said unto the lad that held him by the hand, 'Suffer me that I may feel the pillars whereupon the house standeth, that I may lean upon them.' Now the house was full of men and women, and all the lords of the Philistines were there; and there were upon the roof about three thousand men and women, that beheld while Samson made sport. And Samson called unto the LORD, and said, 'O Lord God, remember me, I pray thee, and strengthen me; I pray thee, only this once, O God, that I may be at once avenged of the Philistines for my two eyes.' And Samson took hold of the two middle pillars upon which the house stood, and on which it was borne up, of the one with his right hand, and of the other with his left. And Samson said, 'Let me die with the Phi,' and Samson said, 'Let me die with the Philistines.'

"And he bowed himself with all his might; and the house fell upon the lords, and upon all the people that were therein. So the dead which he slew at his death were more than they which he slew in his life. Then his brethren and all the house of his father came down, and took him, and brought him up, and buried him between Zorah and Eshtaol in the burying place of Manoah his father. And he judged Israel twenty years."

A Nazarite is an Israelite consecrated to the service of God, under vows to abstain from alcohol, let the hair grow, and avoid defilement by contact with corpses (Book of Numbers, Chapter 6).

God did not approve Samson and Delilah's relationship. Samson made the first mistake by getting with her, because she already had the potential to lead him astray. She had already plotted to lead him directly into their hands. That's exactly what she did. Samson was consecrated to God since birth. He violated the vow that was made to God. He was a lustful man who wanted to satisfy his lustful desires.

36

Samson was called by the Lord to help free the Israelites from the Philistines. Samson's mission would require physical strength. The Lord made a covenant with Samson that as long as he obeyed the Lord, he would be physically strong. Samson's long hair (see Judges 13:5) was a sign of this covenant. He said, "All the days of his vow of separation, no razor shall touch his head. Until the time is completed for which he separates himself to the LORD, he shall be holy. He shall let the locks of hair of his head grow long."

Samson's secret strength was in his hair. God made a covenant with Samson to give great physical strength to his body, to be able defeat the enemies of the Israelites from the Philistines. Samson was strong physically; he was portrayed like a hero to both Israelites and the Philistines. But his lustful desires led him directly into the hands of the Philistines, who wanted to kill him. Let's see how that happened. According to the text in Judges 16, Samson went to Timnah, the Philistines territory. The news spread out fast to the community, by the newscaster: "Hello; Samson is in town. Quick, bring Delilah the harlot to meet him, so that we can kill him! Samson saw Delilah and fell in love with her. Samson's lustful desires led to a romantic attraction to Delilah, which became an unbreakable soul tie.

The pleasure of sin leads to betrayal (because Delilah cut his hair, the source of his strength). Samson disobeyed God's ordinance to stay away from any woman that did not follow the Lord. Delilah was a well-known harlot. The men in the community knew her. They used Delilah, the harlot, to bring the downfall of this man, Samson, whom God had chosen to do his work. She was bad. After she went to bed with Samson, he fall asleep. She called a group of people nearby to come

37

in and tie him up. They gouged out his eyeballs, and then Samson was in pain and blind. They put him to grind grain in the Mills plaza for the public to see. Samson's lack of self-control had led him to self-destruction. Sin is ugly. R. Zacharias said, "**Sin will take you** farther than **you** want to go, keep **you** longer than **you** want to stay, and cost **you** more than **you** want to pay."

Galatians 6:7-8 (NIV) says: "Do not be deceived; God cannot be mocked. A man reaps what he sows. Whoever sows to please their flesh, from the flesh will reap destruction; whoever sows to please the Spirit, from the Spirit will reap eternal life." Delilah betrays this man— tying him up, cutting his hair, gouging out his eyeballs, dragging him down to the Mills plaza to grind grain. The lessons we learned from Samson is that when there is a decline in moral value, a degradation of your character, and disrespect for God, it leads you to experience severe pain and shameful death. If God chose you to do something, obey him. Your reward will be great in heaven. Be smart and be wise, because every decision we make in this life has consequences.

Chapter 4

Clean Your Life with Positive Thoughts

Love Is the Key That Opens the Door to Your Soulmate

Get rid of baggage from your life. Let go of all the negative experiences in your life. Get up, square your shoulders, look straight in front of you and move on. Call on the Lord to help you. God says in his word that he will never leave you nor forsake you. Don't let past romantic failures drag you down. The relationship that didn't work out for you, say goodbye to it. Start a new day tomorrow. Bury the hatchet. Whom are you mad at? Quell that anger because tomorrow is a better day. God will help you recover what you lost. Clean your life with positive thoughts. Focus on the promises of God, and say, "I can do all things through Christ who strengthens me." Prepare your heart to be compatible in finding an excellent person to marry.

If You Are a Good Cook, You Will Find Your Soulmate

Eventually, when you find a soulmate that fits the criteria you are looking for, at one point in your life, you are going to get engaged and then say, "I do!" The Bible says: "An excellent wife, who can find? She is far more precious than jewels. The heart of her husband trusts in her, and he will have no lack of gain. She does him good, and not harm, all the days of her life. She seeks wool and flax, and works with willing hands. She is like the ships of the merchant; she brings her food from afar. She loves and adores her husband, she prepare the meals that he likes, his favorite ones."

Ian Somerhalder says: "The way to a man's heart is through his stomach. "What does that mean? It means that if a woman wants a man to fall in love with her, she needs to be a good cook and to provide him with excellent meals. A man whose belly is satisfied with succulent meals will always want to come home to eat delicious meals, because you are the best at cooking, and nobody can cook like you. Even at work, he will be thinking, what's for dinner tonight? He gets excited to finish his job because he expects to be surprised by a loving wife, someone who is fun to be with and who will spend time with him and make him feel loved and appreciated. We learned that food can be a way to a man's heart. Ladies, it's not hard. We need to polish our cooking skills to make our cooking tasty, and decorate it really well.

You Need to Compliment Your Soulmate for a Job Well Done

This paragraph is addressed to couples or current soulmates that are engaged and want to be married someday. Your man loves to receive compliments from you. When your man fixes a problem in the house, tell him that he is the expert that you can always rely on, and that he is good at everything. Say thank you, and give him a hug. You need to appreciate him, to stand up for him, to care about him and create ways to maintain your relationship in good standard. When he is working, you can text him and say, "I wish you were here right now;

this would have been a cuddling time for the two of us." You really show him you miss him and are thinking about him. "I've felt so protected and safe when I'm with you." Those words melt your soulmate's heart. He will always make time to be with you. These are the words you should never say to your soulmate: "Your mother is coming over." Even if you are joking, never say, "You look fat!" Or, "Don't talk to me!" Never say those words. It creates distrust and lack of confidence on your part. Don't be mean to him; be nice. Tell him or her: "The sun is shining brighter when you are with me. You are so amazing!"

Give Him Undivided Attention When He Is Talking to You

Shut the shutters, put the cell phone away, look your soulmate straight in the eyes, focus on him and listen attentively to what he is saying to you. Being in a relationship is like having a full-time job. You have to give constant attention to your soulmate to nurture the relationship. One way to nurture the relationship is through conversation. When he is talking to you, listen more than you talk. This is how you become emotionally connected with him or her. This is how you would know what makes him happy, what he likes and what causes him pain. That's why it's good to listen. Epictetus says: "We have two ears and one mouth so that we can listen twice as much as we speak." So pay attention to his conversation; let him talk. You need to be respectful of your soulmate.

Celebrate with him when he accomplishes a major milestone in his life, such as being promoted in his job, or receiving a diploma from a graduate school. The biggest mistake you can make is to bring up his past. That will shut him down. I don't even think asking for forgiveness will work. If you fall in love with your soulmate, accept him with all his flaws. Never ever bring up his past. Don't expect to change him either; only God can change somebody's heart. Never rebuke him in front of his friends, your friends or the family. Give him his space. Never give him the silent treatment. Tell him what you want from him. Compliment him often for helping you with the laundry or chopping up vegetables.

Keep working by faith and not by sight. True love is going to find you one day.

Proverbs 22:18 NIV says: "He who finds a wife finds a good thing, and obtains favor from the LORD."

In Song of Solomon 3:4, we find this tender phrase: "I have found the one my soul loves." The Hebrew word translated as "soul" refers to the innermost core of the person; that which gives a person breath and life. It is also the seat of all emotions and passions. The word for "love" here is versatile, but it can refer to romantic love, patriotic love, familial love and love from God.

Different Strategies to Find Your Soulmate

These are some different strategies to find your soulmate. Write your vision on a billboard. Put it in plain sight where you can see it often. Revise often when you accomplish one of your goals, and reward yourself. Be an explorer; read books. Go to the movies, see some Broadway shows and go fishing with your family or friends. Take a walk in the park. Go hiking with friends. Have a barbecue in your backyard; invite your friends and neighbors. You may have some interesting people in your neighborhood that you don't even know about. Be kind to yourself, and love yourself and your neighbors. Reward yourself; you are doing well! Go to a birthday party. Bring some flowers to celebrate with the birthday person. Tell some funny jokes and laugh. The Bible said that "laughter is good medicine," in Proverbs 22:18 (NIV). "A joyful heart is good medicine, but a crushed spirit dries up the bone."

Take a moment and think about how you have been working hard and just trying to make it through the day. Honestly, do you remember the last time you had a good laugh? This is so important. Laughter is proven to make you feel better. If you are anxious, you cannot laugh. Laughter can decrease emotional and physical pain and make you a happier person. Have a good belly laugh (ha ha ha). It will feel like your interior organs are jogging, and you will feel some relief from anxiety and pain. Play a game that brings laughter to you and your playmates. Burst into laughter every chance you get.

Today Is the Day to Make Your Dreams Come True

What is your true goal that you are after? What is your objective that you anticipate and clearly vibrate in your subconscious? What is it that you really want to accomplish? What do you really want? Have you been dreaming about quitting your job and starting your own business, or do you want to start a new job so that you can be more flexible and spend time with your family? You need to set up your goal. Start dreaming. Set up the time to get your equipment together. Write down your plan and put it on the mirror and many other places in the house where you can see it. Set a deadline for the accomplishment of your dream. Reward yourself. You work hard, so you deserve to be rewarded.

Chapter 5

Falling in Love with Your Soulmate – What That Entails

5

You Will Feel More Secure around Your Soulmate

When you fall in love with the right person, you need to make time in your schedule for that person, either to talk, go out for dinner or go to church, and present your "new beau" to your pastor and friends. If your friends have some groups of young people that meet together for Bible study, join them. The more godly back-up support you have around you, the better it is for your relationship. Set up some goals. Sign up for mission trips in different countries around the world. You will get rid of baggage from your life, which ensnared you. Let go of all the negative experiences in your life. Get up, square your shoulders, look straight in front of you and move on. Call on the Lord to help you. God says in his word that He will never leave you or forsake you. You will be surprised at how spiritually grown up you will become; when you trust God, He will step into your situation and make all your dream comes true.

People who are in love, generally feel more secure when they are around their beloved. They feel the other person's pain as their own, and are willing to sacrifice anything for the sake of conquering their love. This young lady, Rebekah, was waiting to meet the man of her dreams. Genesis (NIV) 24:1-67 recounts the history of Rebekah and Isaac: how they find each other, and how they fall in love and get married.

History of Isaac and Rebekah

Abraham was now very old, and the LORD had blessed him in every way. He said to the senior servant in his household, the one in charge of all that he had, "Put your hand under my thigh. I want you to swear by the LORD, the God of heaven and the God of earth, that you will not get a wife for my son from the daughters of the Canaanites, among whom I am living, but will go to my country and my own relatives and get a wife for my son Isaac."

The servant asked him, "What if the woman is unwilling to come back with me to this land? Shall I then take your son back to the country you came from?"

"Make sure that you do not take my son back there," Abraham said. "The LORD, the God of heaven, who brought me out of my father's household and my native land, and who spoke to me and promised me on oath, saying, 'To your offspring, I will give this land,' he will send his angel before you so that you can get a wife for my son from there. If the woman is unwilling to come back with you, then you will be released from this oath of mine. Only do not take my son back there." So the servant put his hand under the thigh of his master Abraham and swore an oath to him concerning this matter.

Then the servant left, taking with him ten of his master's camels, loaded with all kinds of good things from his master. He set out for Aram-Naharaim and made his way to the town of Nahor. He had the camels kneel down near the well outside the town; it was toward evening, the time the women go out to draw water.

The Prayer of Eliezer Abraham's Servant

Then Eliezer Abraham's servant prayed, "LORD, God of my master Abraham, make me successful today, and show kindness to my master Abraham. See, I am standing beside this spring, and the daughters of the townspeople are coming out to draw water. May it be that when I say to a young woman, 'Please let down your jar that I may have a drink,' and she says, 'Drink, and I'll water your camels too,' let her be the one you have chosen for your servant Isaac. By this, I will know that you have shown kindness to my master."

Before he had finished praying, Rebekah came out with her jar on her shoulder. She was the daughter of Bethuel, son of Milkah, who was the wife of Abraham's brother Nahor. The woman was very beautiful, a virgin; no man had ever slept with her. She went down to the spring, filled her jar and came up again.

Rebekah Gives Water to Eliezer Abraham's Servant

The servant hurried to meet her and said, "Please give me a little water from your jar."

"Drink, my lord," she said, and quickly lowered the jar to her hands and gave him a drink.

After she had given him a drink, she said, "I'll draw water for your camels too, until they have had enough to drink." So she quickly emptied her jar into the trough, ran back to the well to draw more water and drew enough for all his camels. Without saying a word, the man watched her closely to learn whether or not the LORD had made his journey successful. When the camels had finished drinking, the man took out a gold nose ring weighing half a shekel, and two gold bracelets weighing ten shekels. Then he asked, "Whose daughter are you? Please tell me, is there room in your father's house for us to spend the night?"

She answered him, "I am the daughter of Bethuel, the son that Milkah bore to Nahor." And she added, "We have plenty of straw and fodder, as well as room for you to spend the night."

Eliezer Gives Thanks to God

Then the man bowed down and worshiped the LORD, saying, "Praise be to the LORD, the God of my master Abraham, who has not abandoned his kindness and faithfulness to my master. As for me, the LORD has led me on the journey to the house of my master's relatives." The young woman ran and told her mother's household about these things. Now Rebekah had a brother named Laban, and he hurried out to the man at the spring. As soon as he had seen the nose ring, and the bracelets on his sister's arms, and had heard Rebekah tell what the man said to her, he went out to the man and found him standing by the camels near the spring. "Come, you who are blessed by the LORD," he said. "Why are you standing out here? I have prepared the house and a place for the camels."

So the man went to the house, and the camels were unloaded. Straw and fodder were brought for the camels, and water for him and his men to wash their feet. Then food was set before him, but he said, "I will not eat until I have told you what I have to say." "Then tell us," Laban said. So he said, "I am Abraham's servant. The LORD has blessed my master abundantly, and he has become wealthy. He has given him sheep and cattle, silver and gold, male and female servants, and camels and donkeys. My master's wife Sarah has borne him a son in her old age, and he has given him everything he owns. And my master made me swear an oath, and said, 'You must not get a wife for my son from the daughters of the Canaanites, in whose land I live, but go to my father's family and to my own clan, and get a wife for my son.' Then I asked my master, 'What if the woman will not come back with me?'

He replied, 'The LORD, before whom I have walked faithfully, will send his angel with you and make your journey a success, so that you can get a wife for my son from my own clan and from my father's family. You will be released from my oath if, when you go to my clan, they refuse to give her to you—then you will be released from my oath.'

"When I came to the spring today, I said, 'LORD, God of my master Abraham, if you will, please grant success to the journey on which I have come. See, I am standing beside this spring. If a young woman comes out to draw water and I say to her, 'Please let me drink a little water from your jar,' and if she says to me, 'Drink, and I'll draw water for your camels too,' let her be the one the LORD has chosen for my master's son.' Before I finished praying in my heart, Rebekah came out, with her jar on her shoulder. She went down to the spring and drew water, and I said to her, 'Please give me a drink.' She quickly lowered her jar from her shoulder and said, 'Drink, and I'll water your camels too.' So I drank, and she watered the camels also. I asked her, 'Whose daughter are you?' She said, 'The daughter of Bethuel son of Nahor, whom Milkah bore to him.'

"Then I put the ring in her nose and the bracelets on her arms, and I bowed down and worshiped the LORD. I praised the LORD, the God of my master Abraham, who had led me on the right road to get the granddaughter of my master's brother for his son. Now if you will show kindness and faithfulness to my master, tell me; and if not, tell me, so I may know which way to turn."

Both Laban and Bethuel Agree to the Engagement of Isaac and Rebekah

Laban, Rebekah's uncle, and Bethuel, Rebekah's father, answered, "This is from the LORD; we can say nothing to you one way or the other. Here is Rebekah; take her and go, and let her become the wife of your master's son, as the LORD has directed." When Abraham's servant heard what they said, he bowed down to the ground before the LORD. Then the servant brought out gold and silver jewelry and articles of clothing, and gave them to Rebekah; he also gave costly gifts to her brother and to her mother. Then he and the men who were with him ate and drank and spent the night there. When they got up the next morning, he said, "Send me on my way to my master."

But her brother and her mother replied, "Let the young woman remain with us ten days or so; then you may go." But he said to them, "Do not detain me, now that the LORD has granted success to my journey. Send me on my way so I may go to my master."

Then they said, "Let's call the young woman and ask her about it." So they called Rebekah and asked her, "Will you go with this man?" "I will go," she said. So they sent their sister Rebekah on her way, along with her nurse and Abraham's servant and his men. And they blessed Rebekah and said to her, "Our sister, may you increase to thousands upon thousands; may your offspring possess the cities of their enemies. Then Rebekah and her attendants got ready and mounted the camels and went back with the man. So the servant took Rebekah and left.

Now Isaac had come from Beer Lahai Roi, for he was living in the Negev. He went out to the field one evening to meditate, and as he looked up, he saw camels approaching. Rebekah also looked up and saw Isaac. She got down from her camel and asked the servant, "Who is that man in the field coming to meet us?"

"He is my master," the servant answered. So she took her veil and covered herself.

Then the servant told Isaac all he had done. Isaac brought her into the tent of his mother Sarah, and he married Rebekah. So she became his wife, and he loved her; and Isaac was comforted after his mother's death.

This history of Abraham, Rebekah, Eliezer Abraham's servant and Isaac, is amazing. This history is full of action; I just love it. Love always wins! Let's recap the history one more time:

Now Abraham was old and well advanced in age, and the Lord has blessed Abraham in all things. So Abraham said to the oldest servant of his house, "Please put your hand under my thigh and I will make you swear by the Lord the God of Heaven and the God of the earth that you would not take a wife for my son from the daughters of the Canaanites among whom I dwell, but you shall go to my country and to my family and take a wife for my son Isaac." And the servant said to him, "Perhaps the woman will not be willing to follow me to this land. I cannot take your son back to the land from which you came." What do I do then if the woman refuses to follow me?"

"You will be released from my old agreement of my master Abraham if you will my God. Then I asked her and said, "Whose daughter are you?" And she said, "The son of Bethuel," and the servant recognized right away that she was related to Abraham. So the servant put the nose ring on her nose, and the bracelets on her wrist. It seems that the nose ring and the bracelets were put on her as a sign of engagement. And he bowed his head and worshiped the Lord and blessed the Lord, the God who had led him in the way of the truth to Miss Rebekah, who was willing to go with him to meet his master. He gave thanks to God for making his mission successful!

When Rebekah Met Isaac, They Fell in Love Right Away

Joy and happiness invades your soul when you fall in love with your soulmate. You will be walking down the street happily skipping from the left foot to the right, and whistling some melodies of love, which comes from deep down in your soul. Your heart will start singing melodies that are brand new to you and may surprise you. She was attracted by this handsome, good looking man, Isaac. She couldn't believe her eyes, the beauty and radiance that manifested by just looking where Isaac stood. Rebekah's eyes popped open, and she said: "Oh, my gosh! He is gorgeous! Is he the ONE for me? I need to take a closer look! I am shaking and trembling here. I have goose bumps all over my body. My heart rhythm is up to the roof! Something is happening! I am falling in love with this man."

"Gosh, I have to do something. I want to laugh; I want to cry—I don't know what to do with myself. Quick, stop the camel," Rebekah said to Eliezer. Rebekah hastily dismounted the camel, and her humble attitude showed respect for the young man that she was going to meet. She instantly covered her head and face with her veil. When Isaac and Rebekah's eyes met, they instantly fell in love with each other. It was love at first sight. Rebekah quickly asked the servant, "Who is this man?" As soon as she heard that it was Isaac, she put on her veil, covering her hair that was hanging down gracefully over her shoulders. Mission accomplished. Isaac and Rebekah had found each

57

other, and they were compatible soulmates; they complemented each other. They fell in love with each other right away. They would be living happily ever after.

When you fall in love, it's like you are walking on the clouds. Yes, walking on the clouds. Love gives you wings. You feel like you want to fly above the clouds. Falling in love makes you feel like you had been sleeping for years, and you finally woke up. The world is smiling at you. The birds join you in singing your melodious love song. I believe that Isaac felt like he was walking on the clouds. He probably had a feeling that something marvelous was going to happen. Usually, in the afternoon, Isaac would take a stroll in the field, as a time of meditation to pray to God and ask for help in finding a suitable wife. That was a familiar place for Isaac to hang out. Isaac went there very often, praying to God and seeking comfort since he had lost his mother, Sarah, three years ago, and he missed her terribly. He would walk in the fields, with a mild wind blowing and messing up his hair. He perhaps prayed Psalms 23:1 (NIV): "The Lord is my shepherd, I shall not want. He makes me to lay down in green pastures. He leads me beside the still waters. He restores my soul." He was meditating on those words when he took a deep breath and looked up. Wow! He saw the camels coming.

Abraham's Prayer

Abraham was called a friend of God in the Bible. He was praying for God to help find a good wife for his son Isaac. Abraham's prayer probably went like this: "Dear God, I am well advanced in age. I am sending my servant to find a wife for my son Isaac. Please send a woman to the well to draw water. The woman that will be kind enough to give a drink of water to my servant, and to water the camels, will be the one that you chose for my son Isaac to marry. You have been faithful to me all my life; you never let me down. You promised that my descendants will be like the stars in the sky, and no one will be able to count them. You promised that my descendants will be like the sand on the seashore.

"I believe your word. O Lord, make it happen today. Give success to my servant; let him bring home the woman that you choose to marry my son Isaac." Abraham knew God's covenant about making Isaac a great nation, and he was concerned about finding Isaac a suitable wife that would follow all the traditions. This woman must not be a Canaanite but someone from Abraham's own relatives. This relationship was bathed in prayer from all the family members. Abraham was praying for Eliezer the servant to go to the well, and he gave him strategies on how to find the right woman to marry Isaac, his son. Isaac, Abraham's son, was praying to find the right woman to marry. I am sure Rebekah was also praying to find the right soulmate. I am sure that Abraham's servants, who walked with the ten camels that came with Eliezer, were also praying for the trip to be successful. I am sure Uncle Laban and Rebekah's father were on their knees very often, praying for Rebekah respectively, their niece and daughter, to find the right man to marry her, because she was twenty-seven years old. This is the example of a praying family that stood together, praying that Rebekah find the right soulmate. I think if you are looking for a soulmate, you should get your parents, friends and your bishop or pastor to pray for you to find your soulmate. Pray to God yourself, for him to open your eyes to see who he wants for you. Have faith in God; He will tell you. Let's go back to Isaac's story.

Isaac's Prayer

Isaac was still praying to God, and bringing to remembrance the goodness and the faithfulness of God toward his father Abraham. He was earnestly seeking God for the servant to identify his future wife. He probably was praying like this: "Lord, I have you; I have everything. You are my all-sufficient God, and all I ever need is found in you. The Lord is my shelter; I shall not want. He makes me to lay down in green pastures. He leads me beside the still waters. He restores my soul." He was meditating on those words, and he took a deep breath and looked up; and lo and behold, he saw a caravan of ten camels coming up the hill. A distinguished, beautiful young lady was riding one of the camels. Isaac probably said, "Thank you, Lord, for answering my prayer by sending me the most beautiful angel I have ever seen."

When you fall in love, your heart starts singing melodies that are brand new to you. A new day has begun for you.

- A new day has begun for you.
- The flowers of the road are smiling at you.
- The birds on the trees seem to welcome you.
- All of a sudden, the world seems to live in perfect harmony, when you fall in love with your soulmate.

Chapter 6

First Find Yourself,
Then Find Your Soulmate

Be Specific In All Your Prayers

To find your soulmate, you need to find yourself first. Who are you? What are you looking for? In all your prayers, you have to be specific.

What Are The Specifics That You Are Looking For In Your Soulmate?

The specifics are: someone who is honest and has a good sense of humor; someone who has a job; someone who shows empathy. You have to bring your petitions to God. Wait on him to respond to you.

Are You Single And Ready To Mingle?

Single and ready to mingle means that a person is no longer in a committed relationship to another person, and so is now looking for another partner. If you are single and ready to mingle, get to know people. The good news is, if you are single and ready to mingle, there are some valuable tips that will help you along the way to find your prince charming. You need to hit the ground running.

You Need To Change Your Wardrobe

Go to the boutique and get some amazing outfits that fit you perfectly. Change your hairstyle, or add new hair color for a more sophisticated look. Be happy with yourself. Wear your favorite outfit to show the outside world that you are single and ready to mingle.

Wear Your New Sexy Outfit to Make Yourself The Center Of Attention

You are rady to date again, so wear your sexy new outfit and show people that you are ready to find someone new, by making yourself the center of attention. Step out with confidence to meet that new person, who may be right around the corner. Go out and be ready to help others and to serve others. Keep smiling; the best is yet to come.

Refresh your fan page and let people know what you are up to. Refresh your fan page; put new pictures and new adventures that will bring some excitement to your audience. For instance, if you have a nice, attractive puppy dressed accordingly, put it on your Facebook. People love to comment on pets. The pet will keep the conversation going.

Go to a five-star restaurant and take a picture of the food that was served to you and which you ate. If you find it delicious, post it on Facebook and your social media. Comment about the restaurant's good services and how delicious the food was. You are going to have many people contacting you to ask for the address of the restaurant. If you are single and ready to mingle, find a friend that you can go out with, who makes you feel less awkward about wanting to find someone who is also looking for someone. That way, you would not feel vulnerable that you are the only one who needs or wants someone in your life, but just that you are two people walking toward the same goals. When you go dancing with a group of females, people readily assume that you are single and looking.

If you get divorced because everything you tried didn't work, stop blaming yourself. It's not your fault; no relationship is perfect, and there's no use dwelling over the things you could have or should have done to stay together. If the other person is not willing to compromise, then you need to let go of that relationship. Refrain yourself from all types of communications that will bring back memories. Remove all his clothes from your sight, and his favorite coffee cup. Stay away from him—no voice calls, no texting, no stalking him online. Don't try to find out what he is doing. Shut him out completely. Do not make any contact with him, which would only bring your pain back that you went through. Focus on yourself; you are still alive and breathing. There is hope for you.

If you were married before, you need freedom before you embark on the great adventure of searching for a soulmate. You have to let go of all the issues that caused your marriage to end. You need to forgive yourself and your spouse for every pain and every outburst of anger that caused emotional pain and mental anguish to each other. It takes some time to clear up those shortcomings. Free yourself of every fear and all anxieties that beseech you, and take steps to move on with your life.

Chapter 7

You Feel Empowered When You Find Your True Soulmate

7

Keep that in mind: You will feel empowered when you find your true soulmate. It's the two of you against the world. You become mentally inseparable. You feel more secure and protected by each other. You are happier than you have ever been, and are strengthened by each other's company.

Your fear and anxiety takes a hike. Suddenly, the world and all around you comes alive. You walk with your head held high. You smile more readily at your neighbors.

How will you know that you have found your soulmate? The soulmate you are looking for can be your best friend. It's a good thing to date somebody you have known over the years. Maybe that person was your classmate, or you met him or her at the workplace. Still, you need to do lots of digging to find out what has been happening for the past few years that you lost contact with them.

You need:

- Someone that you get along with well. Discover if you have the same interests.
- Someone that you can share your thoughts with.

- Someone you can have lots of fun with and share the latest news or the latest romance.
- Someone with a great sense of humor.
- Someone who is the first person you call if something happens to you.
- Someone you can trust and share your joy and happiness together.
- Someone who cares about you.
- Someone who is honest with you.

When you fall in love with your soulmate, these characteristics will be revealed for everyone to see: love, romance, comfort, intimacy, sexuality, spirituality, compatibility and trust.

When God wants you to be with somebody, there will be chemistry between you; there will be happiness and laughter, and both will be thinking the same thought at the same time.

The subject of how to pick up a date should have been taught in school at the appropriate age. Sometimes we blindly pick up somebody, and we rely on chance alone, and we expect it to work. We fail miserably because nobody gives us a "hint" of what to expect in a relationship. Some people meet their soulmate in college. Others grow up in the same neighborhood, where the parents know each other. Some others meet in a seminar for like-minded professionals. Or you could meet in church or when you go on a mission trip. When you go on a mission trip, you have a chance to spend five to ten days in a foreign country with a group of like-minded people. It's like a vacation, with a mission to visit the orphanage, to bring medical necessities to help those that are less fortunate.

Chapter 8

Make Your Health a Priority

Visit Your Medical Doctor Regularly

Make your health a priority by visiting your medical doctor regularly. Keep up with your follow-up appointments. Remain healthy. Eat well. Get a good night's sleep, 7–8 hours per night if you can. Love yourself and be happy.

Schedule A Set Time To Exercise Your Body

Set time for meditation; pray, fast and ask God to forgive you. Take it one day at a time. Just getting through the day before you is more than enough to take on during life after divorce. Seek out support and try to avoid self-isolation. Get counseling through a therapist or your pastor; join a Bible study or support group. Keep things as normal as possible. Keep the children out of it. Take your time, do some traveling. Keep your mind busy. Learn a new language, like Spanish or French. Learn a new skill. Go to college and finish that degree that you've been postponing for several years. Be extra nice; open the door for people that come after you. Visit a church; meet the bishop or pastor, and ask for prayer. Remain present in the moment, and remain positive always.

The Story of Abigail and David

The Bible reports, in 1 Samuel 25:2-42, the history of Abigail and David. Abigail was a beautiful and intelligent woman. She was married to Nabal, who was rich but was a fool. He was a jerk; he was rude and mean in all his dealings. The third character was David, who was anointed by God to become king of Israel. Saul was evil. He was the reigning king at that time, but he would be ousted in God's proper timing, and David would be appointed to reign over the kingdom of Israel. The story of Abigail and David is such a beautiful story. It depicts the character of Abigail, a women of value, and who was faithful, wise, intelligent and gorgeous. Her wise behavior saved her life, her household, her sheep, goats and servants from being totally slaughtered by the soon-to-be King David, because of her foolish husband, Nabal. Let's dive into the story. The story is found in the Bible, in the book of 1 Samuel 25. As we go along, we will read the verses together.

Verses 2-8: A certain man in Maon, who had property there at Carmel, was very wealthy. He had a thousand goats and three thousand sheep, which he was shearing in Carmel. His name was Nabal, and his wife's name was Abigail. She was an intelligent and beautiful woman, but her husband, a Calebite, was surly and mean in his dealings. Abigail, a beautiful woman, married a foolish, mean, alcohol addicted, rich man, and that's the perfect setup for drama down the road. While David was in the desert, he heard that Nabal was shearing sheep. So he sent ten young men and said to them, "Go up to Nabal at Carmel and greet him in my name. Say to him, 'Long life to you! Good health to you and your household! And good health to all that is yours! Now I hear that it is sheep-shearing time. When your shepherds were with us, we did not mistreat them, and the whole time they were at Carmel, nothing of theirs was missing. Ask your own servants and they will tell you. Therefore, be favorable toward my young men, since we come at a festive time. Please give your servants and your son David whatever you can find for them.'"

Why David Was in the Wilderness

David was in the wilderness because he was running away from Saul, who wanted to kill him. He had an entourage of six hundred soldiers, along with wives, children and servants. He was responsible to feed them every day. David was making a celebration and a feast for his entourage group comprised of warriors and family. He sent ten young men to Nabal, the mean, rich man next door to his encampment crew. The ten messengers politely greeted Nabal. Let's see what happens next.

When David's men arrived, they gave Nabal this message in David's name. Then they waited.

Nabal answered David's servants, "Who is this David? Who is this son of Jesse? Many servants are breaking away from their masters these days. Why should I take my bread and water, and the meat I have slaughtered for my shearers, and give it to men coming from who knows where?" David's men turned around and went back. When they arrived, they reported every word.

David's encampment was by Nabal's sheep holding area, separated only by a wall. David could hear, several days in a row, that Nabal's servants were shearing the sheep. What does that mean? Shearing sheep is the process by which the woolen fleece of a sheep is cut off. The purpose is to make money!

Cha-ching! Nabal was making money selling the wool that came from the sheep. So David sent his messenger to Nabal.

This is my commentary on David's message to Nabal: "Hello, I am David, and I am temporarily encamped here, where there is only one wall separating my group and your sheep holding area. My soldiers watch over your sheep always, and prevent thieves and animals from stealing or killing your flock. I am having a celebration. Send me provisions, clothing, food, sheep, goats—anything you can." Nabal answered, "Who is David? The son of Jesse? Are you a runaway who has escaped from your masters? Do you expect me to give my bread, my water and my meat to this dude? I don't even know where you come from. Nabal was selfish and egotistical; he was focusing on his water, his bread, his meat and his shearers. Nabal was probably saying, "David is not allowed to come here." The servants turned back and reported everything to David.

David said to his men, "Put on your swords!" So they put on their swords, and David put on his. About four hundred men went up with David, while two hundred stayed with the supplies.

One of the servants told Nabal's wife Abigail, "David sent messengers from the desert to give our master his greetings, but he hurled insults at them. Yet these men were very good to us. They did not mistreat us, and the whole time we were out in the fields near them, nothing was missing. Night and day, they were a wall around us all the time we were herding our sheep near them. Now think it over and see what you can do, because disaster is hanging over our master and his whole household. He is such a wicked man that no one can talk to him."

David told his soldiers, "Get ready; I need four hundred of you. Put on your sword!"

David put on his sword also. David was going to cause trouble for him. David was going to wipe out Nabal and everything that belonged to him, because he had been so rude, mean and inconsiderate to him. He proved himself to be a fool. Nabal was in trouble; he didn't know that David was a warrior who had never lost a battle. While Nabal was devouring a huge amount of food, and while engaging in binge drinking alcohol, David and his armed soldiers were making their way to Nabal's housing complex. A servant ran to Abigail and told her what was going on.

Abigail lost no time. She took two hundred loaves of bread, two skins of wine, five dressed sheep (cooked and ready to eat) five seah (a unit of dry measure, one-third of a bushel) of roasted grain, a hundred cakes of raisins and two hundred cakes of pressed figs, and loaded them on donkeys. Then she told her servants, "Go on ahead; I'll follow you." But she did not tell her husband Nabal.

As she came riding her donkey into a mountain ravine, David and his men were descending toward her in the same ravine, and she met David there.

David had just said, "It's been useless—all my watching over this fellow's property in the desert so that nothing of his was missing. He has paid me back evil for good. May God deal with David, be it ever so severely, if by morning I leave alive one male of all who belong to him!" When Abigail saw David, she quickly got off her donkey and bowed down before David, with her face to the ground. She fell at his feet and said, "My lord, let the blame be on me alone. Please let your servant speak to you; hear what your servant has to say.

"May my lord pay no attention to that wicked man Nabal. He is just like his name—his name is Fool, and folly goes with him. But as for me, your servant, I did not see the men my master sent. Now, since the LORD has kept you, my master, from bloodshed and from avenging yourself with your own hands, as surely as the LORD lives and as you live, may your enemies and all who intend to harm my master be like Nabal. And let this gift, which your servant has brought to my master, be given to the men who follow you. Please forgive your servant's offense, for the LORD will certainly make a lasting dynasty for my master, because he fights the LORD's battles. Let no wrongdoing be found in you as long as you live. Even though someone is pursuing you to take your life, the life of my master will be bound securely in the bundle of the living by the LORD your God. But the lives of your enemies, he will hurl away as from the pocket of a sling. When the LORD has done for my master every good thing he promised concerning him, and has appointed him leader over Israel, my master will not have on his conscience the staggering burden of needless bloodshed or of having avenged himself. And when the LORD has brought my master success, remember your servant."

I comment on these verses above. Here comes the diplomatic heroine, the one and only "Abigail," who saves the day and prevents the slaughter of her own house and family. Come on Abigail, we count on you; do something. Abigail did not waste time. She perceived that David was on his way to Nabal's house—her house. She was smart, decisive and generous. She called her servants and gave them a heads-up to quickly align some donkeys and load them down with food: raisin cakes, fig cakes, five dressed up sheep (already prepared to eat) and 200 loaves of bread. She sent the provision ahead of herself. Then she rode on her own donkey, and while riding up toward the ravine, David was coming down the ravine with his troop. When she met David, she dismounted the donkey and bowed down to the ground at David's feet. She humbled herself before David and took responsibility for Nabal's foolish behavior. Abigail delivered the most humble, heartfelt plea. She said to David, "It's my fault; I am ready to take the blame for Nabal's selfish behavior." She should be the one to give a reward to David because his soldiers protected Nabal's sheep and flocks from animal attacks and thieves. She understood that her husband behaved like a jerk; he was rude and ungrateful. She appealed to David not to take vengeance, because it wasn't worth it. These are the reasons she gave for not taking vengeance:

a. "This husband of mine does not deserve your time. He is an old brat, a drunkard and good for nothing."

b. "David, you are anointed by God; in the same way you were able to defeat Goliath, God will defeat all your enemies."
c. "Because that old fool hurled insults at you, does not mean he needs to die."
d. "You are the future king. It does not look good to have innocent blood on your hands."

David said to Abigail, "Praise be to the LORD, the God of Israel, who has sent you today to meet me.

May you be blessed for your good judgment and for keeping me from bloodshed this day, and from avenging myself with my own hands. Otherwise, as surely as the LORD, the God of Israel, lives, who has kept me from harming you, if you had not come quickly to meet me, not one male belonging to Nabal would have been left alive by daybreak." Then David accepted from her hand what she had brought him, and said, "Go home in peace. I have heard your words and granted your request."

What a woman! Abigail won over David's heart. David granted her request purely, and simply sent her home. She is a winner. She should have won a Nobel prize for peace. When Abigail went back home, Nabal was in the house holding a banquet fit for a king. He was in high spirits and very drunk. So she did not tell him anything until daybreak. Then in the morning, when Nabal was sober, his wife told him all these things, and his heart failed him and he became like a stone. In my opinion, he probably had a stroke. About ten days later, the LORD struck Nabal and he died.

When David heard that Nabal was dead, he said, "Praise be to the LORD, who has upheld my cause against Nabal for treating me with contempt. He has kept his servant from doing wrong and has brought Nabal's wrongdoing down on his own head." Then David sent word to Abigail, asking her to become his wife. His servants went to Carmel and said to Abigail, "David has sent us to you to take you to become his wife." She bowed down with her face to the ground and said, "Here is your maidservant, ready to serve you and wash the feet of my master's servants." Abigail quickly got on a donkey and, attended by her five maids, went with David's messengers and became his wife.

David said to Abigail, "Praise be to the LORD, the God of Israel, who has sent you today to meet me."

What a loving story with a magnificent ending! This is what a great God can do, the God who is in control of everything—the God who guides your life and always provides you with the best.

Lessons Learned From Abigail

Abigail showed great wisdom in her behavior. She acted quickly and was able to appease the furor of David, and her household was spared from destruction. When she got up from the ground, she was a gorgeous woman, and she was looking straight into David's eyes. Her speech was eloquent; pure wisdom was coming out of her lips. She was brilliant! She apologized for her husband's behavior, and she asked for forgiveness for him. And she blamed herself for Nabal's insult to the king. She was fearless, took control of the situation, evaluated what needed to be done and acted on it right away. She sent her servants ahead of her with food ready to eat. She put herself in harm's way to protect her household and to prevent David from shedding innocent blood. Although she was in a sad marriage, she showed respect to her husband.

Abigail was a true peacemaker. She took quick action and displayed sound judgment and reasoning. She negotiated with David and encouraged him not to shed innocent blood, because God would take care of his enemies. David did not waste time on taking action against his enemy Nabal. He did not know that a surprise was waiting for him. David, coming down the mountain with a sword on his thigh, was ready to fight. Looking down the hills, he saw five donkeys being led by five servants, coming up the hill with all kinds of succulent meals. The roasted lambs permeated the air. I am sure David and his men were hungry. Here it is! A feast was prepared for them by this amazing woman Abigail. Abigail came and bowed down at David's feet. At this point, David probably said to take the sword away from him. David's countenance changed from being a fighter to a person who wanted to forgive. David was shocked at the eloquence of this woman's speech.

How was Abigail able to turn the wrath of the soon-to-be King David, and pacify it? The Bible tells us in Proverbs 16:14 (NIV): "The wrath of the king is a messenger of death, but the wise man will appease it." David must have been thinking about that woman and what she did that day. Her wisdom spared him from shedding innocent blood. David probably said to himself that he would always remember Abigail, because she was honest, fearless and remained faithful to her husband. No matter what, she stood by him and defended him. David became emotionally connected to Abigail. Actually, a woman like her, he would need in his kingdom; he would keep her in his mind. Let all "Abigails" today stand up and shine forth, for your soulmate is looking for you!

Abigail's history started with Nabal. Her chaotic husband's craziness almost cost her life, and she ended up victoriously marrying the soon-to-be King David.

Can the "Abigails" stand up? You are looking for your soulmate, right? Be like Abigail; act like Abigail—love like her, defend others like her, be faithful, be honest, be humble, be thoughtful, be courageous, become a peacemaker and leave the rest to God. He will give you a miracle that will blow your mind!

David the mighty warrior, impeccably dressed with his sword on his thigh, was ready to fight Nabal for his arrogance and mistreatment of David's men. And David and four hundred men (soldiers) were on their way to make him pay for his insult toward David. David's anger was justified because now was the time for vengeance. David was coming to destroy Nabal and anything that belonged to him. David, the soon-to-be king, had never lost a battle! Just one look changed everything. David looked down the mountain, and he saw five donkeys coming up the mountain, carrying the most succulent food for a feast. Closely following was a beautiful woman called Abigail. She was riding on a donkey. Abigail came up the hill and knelt down at his feet. David probably gave her a hand to stand up. Abigail eloquently spoke with David. That was a solemn moment for David. Her speech convinced

David not to shed innocent blood, because he was the soon-to-be king, and she did not want David to have a bad review. David listened to her, sat down with his four hundred men (soldiers) and ate the food. Then David sent Abigail back home. Wow!

The lesson learned from this scenario was that David was a powerful man. He was angry. He had the right to teach Nabal a lesson, but he listened to Abigail's sound advice and let go of his anger, his frustrations, pain, retribution and anxiety—he let go of all that. David ended up marrying Abigail because Abigail had great wisdom. She was honest, and she took the blame for her husband. She displayed sound judgment, which saved her and her household. David's actions can play a role in our lives today—to just let go of any frustrations and move on with our lives!

Chapter 9

Seeking Your Soulmate is a Major Task

9

There Must Be Chemistry Between The Two Of You

It's a major task to find your soulmate; there must be chemistry between the two of you. Having chemistry is a magic feeling that electrifies two people that are in love.

There is a Connection That Draws These Two People Together

They constantly think about each other. They spend time together, either going to the beach during hot summer days, jogging through Central Park on Saturdays or working out in the gym—they are always together. They communicate with each other via email, text, sign language and social media. Communication is very important at the beginning and during a relationship, where two lovers express their love for each other, and their fears, happiness or joy.

Connect with secure groups of friends you are familiar with. Sometimes it's good to go out with a group of friends to watch a movie, a show or go out to dinner. Travel to familiar resorts for vacations. You can go to family resorts with a group of friends' family members, loved ones that you appreciate over the years, and get out and enjoy life. Enjoy yourself; life is good. When you get up in the morning, and the sun is brightly shining, shake off the laziness and seize the day. Talk to God to give you direction for your life. Ask God to give you guidance. The Bible says that the mercy of God is new every morning, so don't miss out. God is always ready with miracles in his hands for you. But you need to access it by praying to God and asking for forgiveness of your sins.

When you make things right with God, you open the door for God's blessings to overtake you. God's presence is available to you 24 hours a day, seven days a week. In Psalms 91:11 (NKJV), it says: "He shall give his angels charge over you to keep you in all your ways. In their hands, they shall bear you up lest you dash your foot against a stone." This is the promise of the Almighty God. God is so good, he assigns an angel to watch over you and to protect the day that you were born. Imagine that! You are God's chosen possession and he cares for you. Love God; talk to him always, and he will lead you to find the love of your life. Be confident; the best is yet to come. God always reserves the best for you. God will not give you any second best. He is working on your soulmate right now and will present him to you. You will be surprised at what the finished product (your soulmate) looks like. "Love is friendship that has caught fire. It is quiet understanding, mutual confidence, sharing and forgiving. It is loyalty through good and bad times. It settles for less than perfection and makes allowances for human weaknesses." – Ann Landers

Read more at https://www.brainyquote.com/authors/ann-landers-quotes

More steps to find your soulmate:

- Be extra nice; open the door for people.
- Help the elderly carry their heavy grocery bags up the stairs. (They probably know people they can refer you to.)
- Go to church, to the altar, and ask the pastor to pray for you.
- Don't leave a church you visited without getting prayed for.
- Go hiking to the top of a mountain; take a deep breath and let go of all your fear, pain and anxiety. Just let them all go.
- During travel time, you can meet somebody—you never know.

How can you find yourself after a breakup? Learn to let go of unwanted baggage, and forgive the person that hurt or betrayed you. Take a deep breath. Take some time for yourself. Go to the gym, exercise and eat well. Have your toenails and your nails done. Make your health a priority. Communicate with others, and connect with other people; nobody is an island. Be present, read some books, be mindful of others, pray and fast if you can. Focus on your well-being.

It's possible that your best friend could become your soulmate. It's easy to find out, because they're your best friend, and you know them. If you are invited to a birthday party, they are the first person you will call and say, "Hey, guess what? I am invited to a birthday party. Do you want to come with me? I don't want to go alone." They will not say no to you; they would cancel other friends' appointments to go with you. They want to keep the relationship going nice and easy, with no drama. If they disagree with something you think of doing, they will tell you right away; they will sit down with you, discuss it, clarify the issue and hammer it down. They are loyal to you.

No competition will be seen between these soulmates. They are deeply connected with each other, and there is no competition between them. As the days go by in that relationship, they become deeply in love and connected, and want to spend the rest of their lives together. They finally realize they belong together, and this relationship gets stronger and stronger every day; nobody else matters.

Seeking a Soulmate is a Major Task

Seeking a soulmate is a major task and a universal necessity for a man or a woman to look into. When the time comes in their lives or they reach a certain age, they start looking for a personal person they can trust; a person who is honest, caring, educated, kind and loving, and a person who is trustworthy and, of course, who has a job and has some money in the bank.

Wikipedia defines soulmate as a person with whom one has a feeling of deep or natural affinity. This may involve similarity, love, romance, platonic relationships, comfort, intimacy, sexual activities, spirituality, compatibility and trust.

What does falling in love with your soulmate entail? There is a type of love that knits together, as one, the very souls of two people (see Malachi 2:15 NIV). "Has not the one God made you? You belong to him in body and spirit. And what does the one God seek? Godly offspring. "So be on your guard, and do not be unfaithful to the wife of your youth."

When you find your true soulmate, both of you become mentally inseparable.

Together, you and your soulmate are ready to conquer the world. King Solomon was the wisest man in the Bible. His wife described about finding her mate for her soul. Read "Song of Solomon," Chapter 3:1-4: "It was but a little that I passed from them, but I found him whom my soul loveth; I held him, and would not let him go, until I had brought him into my mother's house, and into the chamber of her that conceived me. To find your soulmate, sometimes you need to find yourself first. You can ask yourself some questions, such as "where am I at right now?"

Taking a peek into the Song of Songs almost feels like you're reading something too intimate to be shared. And yet, God included this poetic book in the Bible to show us how true love in marriage is honorable to the Lord. Reading through the Song of Songs, one cannot help but understand, and long for, the depth of such intimate oneness expressed in this biblical account. When you find your soulmate, it's going to be like you are united against the world. You two will be mentally inseparable. You feel secure and protected when you are with your soulmate.

The first quality to seek in a soulmate is generosity. Are they emotionally stable? Does this person cares for himself?

For bonuses go to ...

Is Your Soulmate Committed to You?

Do you both see the world with the same eyes? Does your soulmate support your passions and decisions? A true soulmate adds value to your life. Soulmates are willing to compromise. Finding your soulmate is basically finding that one person (like finding a needle in a haystack). During your soulmate search, you have to find a person whom you can put up with, and who, on the other hand, can put up with you. Go ahead and start scanning heaven and earth; start searching high and low to find this amazing person that you can put up with, and who will accept you as you are, including your failures.

> *"Love isn't something you find.*
> *Love is something that finds you."*
> – Loretta Young

Love should be the primary reason why you are searching for your soulmate.

Soulmates don't judge each other; they encourage you to be better. You show respect for each other. You have extreme empathy for them. You feel calm around them. You share the same life goals.

Spiritually speaking, God created you in your mother's womb. He knows you very well. He breathed the breath of life into your nostrils as your mother pushed you out into this world. God was at the scene and said you shall live; and you started breathing. When you hear the first cry of the newborn, the lungs expand, and the baby can inhale and exhale on his own. The baby's lungs start functioning properly. It's a new life. There is hope for the family, the society and even the world. The whole family rejoices because a brand new baby is born. That baby has a body, a mind and a soul that is maintained and renewed by his heavenly father, God. This baby has a soul. God already chose a soulmate partner for that baby. It's a big world, but someday by chance, that baby will grow up to become a young man, and will meet the soulmate that was created for him. And that will be the perfect match created just for you. It is said that even before you were born, your true spiritual soulmate is the person God has intended to help you complete each other while living on the earth.

A person is unable to complete his mission in life alone. Everyone needs someone to help them become a better person. If you are an honest, sincere and committed soulmate, your relationship helps you to become a better version of yourself. You have to push yourself beyond your comfort zone, and beyond your limits to find your better self.

Even though we tend to think as a soulmate, relationships can be rough at the beginning. Your relationship can be like a puzzle made of five hundred pieces that you are trying to click into place. Sometimes it looks like you do not fit together at all, but soon after a little bit of twisting, turning and flipping the pieces around, you feel the moment of the perfect click. It's a feeling deep in your soul, which says that this is the right one.

You might not be physically attracted to each other when you first meet, but there is a mysterious force pushing you forward that tells you this is the right one for you. In the book of Genesis, 1:26 (NIV), it says, "And God said, let us make man in our image, after our likeness, and let them have dominion over the fish of the sea, and over the fowl of the air, and over the cattle, and over all the earth, and over every creeping thing that creepeth upon the earth.

"So God created man in his own image, in the image of God created he him; male and female created he them. And God blessed them, and God said unto them, be fruitful, and multiply, and replenish the earth, and subdue it: and have dominion over the fish of the sea, and over the fowl of the air, and over every living thing that moveth upon the earth. In the garden where God created Adam, He said, "It is not good for men to be alone."

The book of Genesis 2:19-25 (NIV) says, "It is not good that the man should be alone; I will make him an help meet for him. And out of the ground, the LORD God formed every beast of the field, and every fowl of the air; and brought them unto Adam to see what he would call them, and whatsoever Adam called every living creature, that was the name thereof.

"And Adam gave names to all cattle, and to the fowl of the air, and to every beast of the field; but for Adam, there was not found an help meet for him. And the LORD God caused a deep sleep to fall upon Adam, and he slept, and he took one of his ribs, and closed up the flesh instead thereof; and the rib, which the LORD God had taken from man, made he a woman, and brought her unto the man.

"And Adam said, 'This is now bone of my bones, and flesh of my flesh: she shall be called woman, because she was taken out of man.'

"Therefore shall a man leave his father and his mother, and shall cleave unto his wife: and they shall be one flesh."

This book is talking about how to find a soulmate. According to the verses you just read, the Garden of Eden is a blissful place that God created for Adam, the first man that God made by using the dust of the soil. God created everything on earth—the ocean, the river, the animals big and small, the birds, the trees, the flowers, and the moon and the stars in the sky. He created Adam to take care of the garden and to give a name to everything that He created. Adam performed his duties during the day. In the afternoon, he would go to the water brooks to refresh himself, but he had nobody that looked like him to share his dream. I came to the conclusion that Adam was lonely. God called Adam and put him into a deep sleep without anesthesia. He performed surgery on Adam. How did He do it? God remove one of Adam rib and formed a woman from it. The name of the woman was Eve. God brought the woman to Adam.

Adam was so excited to see another being that would complete him. He said, "WOW," and that was the origination of the word "woman." The first wedding originated in the Garden of Eden, and was performed by God, when God brought the woman to Adam. Can you believe that all the animals, the water brooks, the fish in the ocean, the butterflies, the eagles, and the giraffes with the long necks that can be seen from far away, all were in attendance of the wedding, and would shout together, AMEN! They started dancing and rejoicing over the most blissful wedding they had ever attended. How romantic that was!

Helen Keller said, "The best and most beautiful things in the world cannot be seen or even touched; they must be felt with the heart."

Ecclesiastes 4:12 says, "And if one prevail against him, two shall withstand him; and a three-strand cord is not quickly broken." You wonder what Adam and Eve did in the garden to entertain themselves. They had organic food from the trees and inside the earth. They could pull the carrots, and gather lettuce, celery, tomatoes and cucumber, and enjoy a big salad for lunch. For dinner, they could catch fish from the ocean, and cook it on the fire that they made. For drinking, cold icy water was within their reach. All kinds of fruits were available to them. I suppose they could go to flower shows during the day. They could play with the animals. It must have been fun to live in the garden. Can you believe that in the garden, everything was provided for free? The above verse said, A three-strand cord does not break easily." What that means in this story is that when God tied the knot, the Triune God was present. The Father, the Son and the Holy Spirit were present when God officiated the wedding of Adam and Eve. After you find your soulmate, invite God to your wedding. Any wedding needs God as your sole foundation, which will pour out his blessings on you and your family.

Ephesians 5:25: "For husbands, this means love your wives, just as Christ loved the church. He gave up his life for her."

Genesis 2:24: "Therefore, a man shall leave his father and his mother and hold fast to his wife, and they shall become one flesh."

Adam's duty in the garden was to know God, to love him, revere and serve him. That was their supreme obligation. For we came forth from him; we are indebted to him for all that makes us what we are, owing all our faculties of every kind to his creative power. We have been sustained in being every moment by his Divine visitation; we have been enriched by him with everything we possess, our hearts and our lives owing to his generous kindness, all their joys and all their blessings; it is in him that we live and move and have our being; we sum up all obligations, we touch the height and depth of exalted duty, when we say that "he is our God." Moreover, all this natural obligation is enhanced and multiplied manyfold by all that he has done for us, and all that he has endured for the salvation which is in Jesus Christ his son.

Adam was to give the deepest and purest satisfaction to God, who has giving to him the most self-denying love; it is also to lead those for whom we have the strongest affection in the way of wisdom, in the paths of honor, joy and eternal life.

Strengthen your personal relationship with God.

Love God first before your partner. All praise, glory and honor belong to God.

Fear the Lord, pray for each other, pray together, go to church and study God's word together.

Ask God to help you change your bad attitudes.

Encyclopedia Britannica describes Agape, Greek agapē, in the New Testament, **the fatherly love of God for humans,** as well as the human reciprocal love for God. In Scripture, the transcendent agape love is the highest form of love between God to men, and men to God (John 3:16 NIV), a verse that is often described as a summary of the message. *Agape* is the word used for the love that moved God to send his only son for the world's redemption. The term necessarily extends to the love of one's fellow humans, as the reciprocal love between God and humans is made in one's unselfish love of others.

You could get married in three minutes in front of two witnesses and someone with the authority to declare you legally married. You don't need a cake, you don't need champagne, you don't need a room full of spectators and you don't need music or even a wedding dress.

You probably need a license and, of course, someone who wants to spend the rest of his life with you. That's important. I am inserting this paragraph to address a couple that are madly in love and can't imagine living life without each other. But you are also reading this book because you have decided that you need someone else at the wedding. At some level, you understand that a wedding between two people, an officiant, and two or even two hundred witnesses is certainly legal, possibly romantic and definitely can be done. However, "Unless the Lord builds the house, we labor in vain," says the Bible

(Psalm 127:1). When two people get married, difficulties will come, and that's why you'll want to invite God from the very beginning, so that when trouble comes, you will be able to ride out the storms. A spiritual wedding begins with spiritual preparation. It's not just about picking hymns and choosing readings from the Bible. It's about preparing your own heart to be as emotionally and spiritually ready as possible, so that when the big day comes, you are confident that God is with you.

When you are ready to meet your soulmate, try to find yourself first.

How do you find yourself after a divorce? When you hear the word "divorce," it evokes in you a great amount of fear, pain and tears, and low self-esteem, worthlessness, of yelling and courtrooms, unhappy kids yelling and fighting with each other because of fear of losing their mother and father, their providers. The kids are sad, and they are angry; they think they are the cause of the separation. Divorce is messy and devastating for the family, and life changing; it takes a toll on the children, families, friends and neighbors as well.

This book focuses on finding a soulmate, and sometimes people that are looking for a soulmate, come from a messy divorce, a heart wrenching breakup with their boyfriend or girlfriend, or even a single person who has never fallen in love before. There are different ways to handle these situations, but they all fall under the same category to find the right soulmate. Divorce takes you by surprise, but it does not kill you. A couple that has gone through a divorce needs time to grieve the loss of intimacy and the habits formed between them. It feels like something was cut off, or even that death has taken place. They need time to grieve and to restart all over if they wish. Can a man live without a woman? Ideally, a man is incomplete without a woman. It can be a mother, a sister, a friend, a girlfriend or wife! Although the male ego does not acknowledge this fact, every man goes through a phase in life where the absence of a woman will be strongly felt. Nothing can beat a "hug filled with love and compassion" coming from a woman, and every man needs this. I don't care how many male friends a man has, there is something magical about a loving woman, her touch, her smile, her aura, her inspiration and the transformation that occurs when a woman touch you. Don't miss out! The need for love is held out to every human being in the universe.

The most fundamental, basic human need is *the need for love*.

A man needs a woman, and vice versa! We are biologically designed the way we are for a reason: to complement one another. According to Maslow's hierarchy of needs (cited by 2075-1), under the physiological needs, these are the biological requirements for human survival: air, food, drink, shelter, clothing, warmth, sex and sleep. Humans in general abide by these principles for a happy life. If a woman declares her need for a man and says that, until she finds the right relationship, she's likely going to be miserable and will probably walk around with a chronic feeling that something is missing from her life. She might be encouraged to take some time alone and learn how to make herself happy. Anytime you feel confused in life and don't know what to do, just pray and ask for God's guidance to help you. He will come through for you.

If a man talks about how much his happiness and ability to succeed in this world rests on the steady love he receives from his wife, it's romantic. If anybody feels that they are not complete without a romantic partner, and wants to dedicate the majority of his or her time to finding that connection, it's a normal behavior. If a woman declares her need for purposeful work, close friendships, creative pursuits, money, sex, more sleep, adventure, etc., she can expect to receive support. It's considered completely all right to honor your needs for all the aforementioned endeavors—in fact, not only that, but it is essential to your health. If you neglect one of these needs, like purposeful work, for example, it goes without saying that you'd likely be less happy, and you'd probably walk around with a chronic sense that something was missing. Learn to be happy by yourself. God is with you always; you are never alone.

After a divorce, the people who loved and supported you when you were married, depart from you. You could look all over for support, but they are gone, and they may even broadcast horrible things about you. Your friends circle becomes smaller, and you are in the process of looking for new friends that you can count on.

A divorced person learns to live a lonely life again. Those divorced men or women who experienced emotional or physical abuse, feel relieved to have finally found a way to escape their hellish situation, where they had no peace, love or joy. After the grieving process is over, like a bird, they are ready to fly to higher heights, and to fly like an eagle again. You may need to strike a balance to adjust in your "single" world. You may need to learn to cook for one person again, balance a budget or shop for groceries. Visit a new church where the congregants don't know anything about you. Make sure you get to hear the word of God, which will comfort you during this time of singleness. You need as much comfort and encouragement as possible to keep you going on with your life. Word of caution: Be careful what you tell your church friends about your messy divorce, because church people gossip a lot. Be encouraged and take it one day at a time. Pray to God, forgive yourself and forgive your ex-husband, and bring all your pain, anxieties and sleepless nights to God. He will take care of you. The day will come when you will be soaring like an eagle with love in your heart!

Where can you go to find your soulmate? These are places you can go to meet people. For example: at the gym, at the library, in apartment buildings, at the airport, in the waiting room of a doctor's office, online, grocery stores, on public transportation, at Macy's, at the jewelry store, at a restaurant, at a stadium, at movie theaters, at baby showers or weddings, while walking in Central Park, at a street fair, at garage sales, at a friend's barbecue, at the beach, while walking your dog, at museums, in parking lots, at coffee shops, at the bank, marathon departure and arrival places, horseback riding, playing golf, visiting Disney World, visiting Canada, visiting waterfalls, flower shows, dog shows. Go to a famous restaurant and sit by yourself. You never know who might ask your permission to share your table. Walk your beautiful puppy; put sunglasses and a nice pink bow on your dog. Walk slowly; you want to hear the compliments.

Be extra nice and open doors for people.

How do you find that special someone who shares your common beliefs, someone that shares your common interests? Is it somebody you can trust? Does that person have a job? Are they financially stable? Is this person single? It's so important to understand that there's a process you have to go through before you can be with your "soulmate." There are two types of relationships: one that you put yourself in, and one that God puts you in. In that light, there are also two types of marriages: one that God has put together, and one you have put together. It goes back to the verse Mark 10:9: "Therefore what God has joined together, let no one separate." So if God isn't in the picture, then of course people will get in the way, and guess what? They'll prosper. In this verse, it's not talking about the physical thought of two people being together, but the spiritual side of your relationship—the soul tie. There are godly soul ties that no man can break. Why is that so?

Jeremiah 29:11 says: "Before I formed you, I knew you," which means that your spiritual being existed before you manifested into the physical in your mother's womb. So your soulmate was with you when God formed you, as Genesis 2:22 says: "The LORD God made a woman from the rib he had taken out of the man, and he brought her to the man." But you guys separated when you manifested into the physical, and at God's timing, you will be reunited. This is why, when you do meet your soulmate, several thoughts will come across your mind, and one of them will be, "I feel like I've known this person all my life." The truth is that you have, in the spiritual realm.

I hope I haven't confused any of you. But honestly, the Bible is so interesting when things begin to link together. It makes me feel like a little kid that can't contain their excitement.

There has to be some sort of chemistry, but don't get it twisted; to identify if someone is your soulmate, it isn't just based on "chemistry," because you can have chemistry with other people. But chemistry is a sort of "firecracker" to lead you to the next 3 keys, so it's needed.

There has to be a connection. There has to be something that draws you to them. Maybe this is wanting to know them more. Don't get it twisted; just because he/she is saved, and they love God and all that, it doesn't mean they are your soulmate. This connection is spiritual; it's because of the soul tie I mentioned before. This connection has to be "godly." It's not created by "something happening" in terms of kissing or having sex with that individual. For example, "After we kissed, I felt like there was something, like a spark!" You need to understand that the connection is not created by something happening; it's always been there, but you're yet to discover that when you meet your soulmate.

You must be whole. Too many times, people jump into relationships feeling incomplete, hurt and even lonely, which are feelings that you know you have to deal with. You haven't got to a stage where you feel whole, where every broken piece is complete, and where you are comfortable being by yourself, and that if given the option to be single for the rest of your life, you honestly wouldn't mind. You have to deal with your own insecurities as well as any other things you need to deal with. You need to surrender all your failures to God. Let him mend your heart and heal you completely, and then you will be on your way to recovery. You can expect a fruitful relationship when you fall in love again. A soulmate doesn't fill a void! The thing about soulmates is that you seeking them out is like telling God you are ready, but let's get it straight—only God knows when you're ready! Maybe God wants to elevate you on an even higher level, so that you and your soulmate are on the same level. Let's go to **Genesis 2:23: "The man (Adam) said, "This is now bone of my bones and flesh of my flesh; she shall be called 'woman,' for she was taken out of man." Verse 21 says: "So the LORD God caused a deep sleep to fall upon the man, and he slept; then He took one of his ribs and closed up the flesh at that place."** God performed surgery on Adam, without anesthesia.

This raises the question: If Adam was asleep when God took out his rib and made Eve, how did Adam know that Eve was his bones and flesh of his flesh? It goes back to what I mentioned before, that when you meet your soulmate, there's that godly connection that you instantly feel, and it's like you've met the other part of you that was missing. This is a profound concept, and God needs to be part of the equation to make a relationship work properly.

There has to be divine confirmation. Look for divine confirmation, which will come from God when you open your Bible. You will find some promises from God, which will confirm exactly what God wants you to do. See if they actually are your soulmate. Then, of course, God will confirm through people and maybe situations to reassure you. Do you have a word from God?

When God approves your relationship, you will feel the presence of God when you're together.

Do not tolerate someone who doesn't see your worth or value. God thinks highly about you and wants you to be happy. God is your father, and you are his prized possession. He is watching over you. He will not give you second best. So get up, look up to God and ask for his help. He will pull you out from that emotionally drained relationship. Go to God in prayer, and let him know how you feel. He will give you another chance.

Don't forget about Adam's rib, although for some people, it seems to be very hard to find their compatible soulmate. God using Adam's rib to form Eve, was the first and only surgery done on a man to create a woman. Let's go to Genesis 2:21-23 NIV): "So the LORD God caused the man to fall into a deep sleep; and while he was sleeping, he took one of the man's ribs and then closed up the place with flesh. Then the LORD God made a woman from the rib he had taken out of the man, and he brought her to the man. The man said, 'This is now bone of my bones and flesh of my flesh; she shall be called woman, for she was taken out of man.'" In this scenario, Adam and Eve are compatible with each other; both are made from the same material. They belong to God. God made them and put them together. They had all they needed to have a successful relationship.

Rebekah feeling the nudge of the Holy Spirit to go to the well to draw water at this particular time, depicts the sovereignty of God moving in her life to bring her the right man that she was waiting for.

Trust God; He is moving behind the scenes to bring to you the right soulmate, the love of your life!

This is a monologue of a woman who is walking her beautiful puppy called Princess:

Today is a beautiful day; no matter how busy you are, you win. Sonia decided to walk in the park with her puppy, Princess. She started talking to her puppy. "How cute you are, Princess. Come on, Princess, you have to help me. Let's go to the park, you beautiful thing. You look amazing."

A man approached Sonia and said, "My name is Justin. How long have you had this cute puppy? What is her name? She looks so cute! This is the prettiest thing I have ever seen. I love that pink sweater that she is wearing. Que linda (Spanish translation means beautiful!)! Wow, look at those shoes. They are beautiful shoes that the puppy is wearing. Wow! This puppy is ready for the winter. You are protecting her from getting sick, and you have done a good job! It looks like Princess is ready to go to a party." (By the way, you can tell that person who owns the dog, that it was so nice to meet them today.) Justin asked politely to take a picture for her, with Princess. The conversation continued between Sonia and Justin. They talked about the weather and how nice it is to take a walk alone and with your cute puppy.

"It's amazing! I wonder if you live in my neighborhood. Where do you live? Do you live in that building over there? Oh, my gosh! This is my favorite place to walk by every day when I'm jogging, and it's such a delight to meet you today, and such a beautiful day. I would like to continue to walk around to enjoy the weather; it's so nice and cozy."

A dog is the best friend man can have. A dog does not get tired or bored with its owner; they want to be by their side and run the show.

"You enjoy her. Princess is very playful; if you throw a ball at her, she picks it up with her teeth or kicks it back to you. Now you can run it back to her. There are so many things dogs can do these days."

"Princess has a dog house, and she has a special chair. She has her own special table and a nice cozy warm bed too. She is very respectful and would not break anything. She knows when she needs to go to the toilet. Princess loves me."

"How long have you had that dog?"

"I have had her for three years. This type of dog doesn't grow taller or longer. Some of the dogs grow a little longer, but not this one. I live in a house by myself."

This is where you can ask a question: What happened? Were you married before? Do you have somebody that you are dating? You can ask all kinds of questions now that you have introduced yourself. You can ask how they are, and be friendly. Justin and Sonia continued to talk for a while. "Would you order food in, go out or do you prefer to cook at home since you live by yourself?"

The food question is perfectly all right to ask your new friend. You can ask if they like to do exercise, and if they have been going to the gym lately. You can continue by asking what they do for a living. You can tell them that you go to the beach if the weather is nice and if it is a hot day, and that sometimes you just chill. Or sometimes you just go hiking. There are so many things to do and so many activities. During the summer, you can meet up with people. You can go together as a group. You can go to a farm and pick apples.

I love life. Life is good. I love to enjoy myself by being with my friends and watching a good movie. I am not too sure what to change about myself, but I know I need to continue my education. What type of education? I know I need to get a master's degree in business. Do you have some passions—something you want to accomplish in life? What would you like to change? Do you want to get a bigger place one day because you planned maybe to have children, and your place is too small for that?

When you are going out with your soulmate, try to connect. Ask questions: Is everything going well for you? What have you been doing lately? What makes you happy and what makes you sad? You've got to ask the right questions. Generally, start talking about the weather; talk about how the weather is nice today, and that you might like to have some ice cream—things like that. Ice cream questions would make you seem more interesting. They should be simple but not boring. You should also have good listening skills. You have to listen, and you have to be active. You can hide your attractive qualities if you ask ambiguous questions. Ask what kinds of physical activities your soulmate likes doing. Do they like going to the gym to work out, or swimming? Do they like to feel strong and healthy?

Around the holidays, like Christmas, New Years and Thanksgiving, if you don't have a special friend to go out with, you can go out with a group of your friends. Go out with people and enjoy yourself; have a good time. You can also go to a show, to a movie theater, different concerts or museums—you never know when you are going to meet somebody, so be nice to yourself. Go out once or twice a week; dress up nicely, put on your lipstick and wear your high heels. Go to a restaurant with your friends and have a good time. If you see an old lady, open the door for her. Hold the door until she has completely gone out the door. You don't know who's watching you, or who's paying attention, and you have to put yourself out there like somebody who is very loving, caring and empathetic. You want to leave a good impression.

A relationship started when Johnny A. (Kiki), a 23-year-old male, was my college classmate. He was kind, jovial, loved to laugh and would joke around, and he showed great respect for young ladies. I overheard that his birthday was coming up the next weekend. Maria, my friend, had a crush on him but kept it hidden. Maria was going to surprise him with a birthday party. She got up early that Saturday morning. She ordered some fried chicken, French fries, sandwiches, balloons of all colors, a few bottles of Coca Cola, plates, cups, ice and salads. Jennifer had a boom box (a portable radio), so she lent it to Maria. Music started to fill the building where Maria lived. At 11 a.m., Maria's room was filled to capacity with college students. The news spread around the campus like wildfire, and all the students came crashing in. Kiki came with his friends, and he was really surprised. He found out that Maria had thrown the party for him, and he was very happy. He danced a lot with Maria. They discovered each other through an act of kindness, and ever since that time, Kiki and Maria were inseparable friends. Two years later, they both graduated with an MBA in business. They got good jobs and started working. One year later, they got married, and they lived happily ever after.

You are very special in God's sight, and God has a plan for you, so be happy and remain positive—the world is yours!

Let me know, if tomorrow was your last day on earth, what you would do today.

I would get up in the morning, say my prayers and read from my Bible. I would say the sinner's prayer. I would want to ask God to forgive me for all my sins, and for everything that I've committed that's not right in his sight. I would ask if it's really the time for me to go, to see if he would change his mind. I would ask for another chance in life. I would ask for 30 more years to live down here on earth. "Dear God, I promise you I will do everything right if you grant my request. I will obey every command I receive from you. I will never ever break your heart again. In Jesus' name, Amen."

I would call everybody that I've done wrong to, and turn things around if given another chance in life. I would forgive those who hurt me. I would make several different phone calls to ask for the forgiveness of those people that I have hurt. I would nicely apologize to my family and friends for the way that I mistreated them. I would sit down with them and say, "Hey! I love y'all, and I'm sorry for everything that I've done wrong to you. I request that you remember me for all the good times that we have had together, and to cast away everything that I did wrong toward you—cut it off and let it go. Forgive me. I would know that you have forgiven me if you cook my favorite food tonight. Let's celebrate family and friendship restoration. Let's have a party tonight. Go ahead and surprise me with my favorite food that I love to eat. This is a partial list of my favorite foods: lobster tails, crab cakes, caviar, paella, sweet potato pie, cheese cake, fried sweet plantain, baked macaroni with four different kinds of cheese, griots (fried pork), litchi chinensis (fruit) and cucumber salad, summer rolls, fish teriyaki, fresh summer garden salad, and many more. Family and friends, bring your friends with you. I will see you tonight at 8:00 p.m. at my house; you know the address. By the way, the restaurant, "Pink Horizon," will provide drinks and dessert. Come on; come all! We are going to have lots of fun tonight."

So it came to pass that lots of guests showed up, and I had a wonderful time. I felt free in my conscience; I felt light. It seemed that a burden was lifted off me. There is nothing like forgiveness. It felt like I was walking on the clouds. I went around the room hugging my guests and shaking their hands, and giving hope again to each other. In the next few weeks, this sudden orchestrated party was the talk of the town, and it would be remembered for years to come.

Can You Hear the Music of the Birds?

I like to take a walk where there is still water, and I like to throw small pebble at the surface of the water. The location where the stone sinks always brings about a "ripple effect" at the surface of the water. I would take time to hear the birds singing. I love the music of the birds. I think you would hear one bird start singing, and then it sets the tone for other birds to join in. Before you know it, you have harmonious sounds of birds singing—the whole orchestra in unison, glorifying God. In the Bible, it says that when the birds sing like that, they are giving glory to God. Believe it or not, every single thing in nature, by their attitude and by their action, can be pictured singing in harmony and glorifying God. When you see the wind blowing and the trees clapping their branches, they are glorifying God. There is a verse in the Bible (Isaiah 55) that says: "For ye shall go out with joy, and be led forth with peace; the mountains and the hills shall break forth before you into singing, and all the trees of the field shall clap their hands." One can see the truth in that—the trees are clapping their hands; they are glorifying God. Take time to appreciate nature, because nature speaks to us.

Whether it's summer, fall, winter or springtime, God is speaking to us. Every day, God has a message for you and me, whether we can hear it or not. Make peace with God; you are his child, and he cares about your well-being, regardless of what you do, good or bad. His message for you is still the same: He loves you.

God is powerful. The way He communicates with me never fails. He downloads instructions into my mind by the leading of the Holy Spirit that lives in me. You may say, "Wait, I think you are crazy!" No;

if you know God, He will reveal himself to you in his own ways. God is mighty. He is holy, and He will be faithful to me every day of my life until I enter His glory. Are you ready to hear God's voice and do what He wants you to do, to help you find your soulmate? Assuming your answer is yes, God is in the process of mending this person's life, fixing him up and even purging him of negative influences and bad habits. By the time God releases that person to you, you will be surprised and will say that only God could do this.

While you are waiting for your victory to come through, work on yourself. Be kind to yourself, love yourself, be nice to people and find God for yourself. Put God on the throne of your life; praise him, adore him, go to church, be friendly, help others, read the Bible and pray every day. Talk to God like you are talking to your friend. God is not far from you at all. Start talking to Him, and start to know his heart. Submit your cares and concerns to Him. God will surprise you with the very best soulmate you could ever imagine. You will rejoice, dance and shout: "ONLY GOD COULD DO IT."

There has been a blockage in the messages that God has been sending to you since the day you took residence on this earth, which belongs to him. Psalms 24:1-2 (KJV) reads: "The earth is the **LORD's**, and the fullness thereof; the world, and they that dwell therein. For He hath founded it upon the seas, and established it upon the floods." God is the Lord of all; He is the King of all kings and Lord of all lords.

Yet He has great concerns about you. When are you going to make the decision to follow Him so that He can open the gate of heaven and download his messages of love, caring blessings and spiritual provisions, which you have been missing for so long? In the Bible, God says, "Seek me and you will find me, when you seek me with all your heart." He wants to tell you that He loves you more than anything.

Every snowflake that comes down is different from each other; God is such a great artist. He has perfected each one of them. **Isaiah 1:18 (NIV)** says: **"Come now, let us reason together, says the LORD: though your sins are like scarlet, they shall be as white as snow; though they are red like crimson, they shall be as wool."** All of these snowflakes show that God is in charge of everything. As for me, I don't know how to make a snowflake; I don't have the equipment to make it, but God does. I cannot make the wind blow, but God can. When the wind blows softly on your face on a hot summer day, you take a deep breath to really enjoy the freshness of that air, deep down into your lungs. It feels good. Other times, the wind starts blowing fiercely and strongly, and transforms itself into a "monster hurricane," which destroys people's houses, uproots trees, floods the streets and destroys cars. But you can say that when all hell breaks loose, God is still in control. He makes all those things happen. God will always put a stop to any bad things that happen in your life, because He can. He controls everything on earth and in heaven. He knows what He's doing because He has the world in his hands.

Here are the basic steps you need in order to find your soulmate:

a. Widen your scope for meeting new people in your life, every week.
b. Keep an open mind to know when you have found someone who could be the one.
c. Develop healthy relationship habits, and keep your soulmate with you for life.
d. Find that your soulmate loves you, and he will be there to walk with you through life, side by side.
e. While you are waiting to find that soulmate, work on yourself first.
f. Clean up your act, and develop a good sense of humor.
g. Start on the same page in life; you are ready for the adventure to find your soulmate.

Every day, money is flowing from somebody's hands, into somebody else's hands. Money is flowing from your boss to your checking account, if you are working. Money is flowing from health insurance to the hospital or the medical clinics. Money is moving from my pocket to the supermarket, and to pay bills. Money transactions are taking place every day around the world. Every day, there is a new love story that just happens or is in the process of happening. We make changes every day. We make choices in our hearts because we know we're alive and well, and we know that we have a new beginning. Every day, changes are being made. Every day, somebody wins the lottery, and they make several millions of dollars. Every day, people are born; and every day, people die. Life is happening right in front of our eyes. I took a long drive to a dog show this afternoon. I came home, jumped in the shower and afterwards sat in my La-Z-Boy chair. What's on TV, I ask myself? I doze off a little bit while drinking a glass of fresh lemonade and strawberry juice. The plan for tonight is to go for dinner with my friends and some family members.

Conclusion

We establish in detail different strategies applicable in this book, to help bridge the gap of finding your soulmate. Actually, you are about to embark upon the greatest adventure of your life! This is the right book for you: *Find Your Soulmate*. Be prepared to smile. Mother Theresa said, "Let us always meet each other with a smile, for the smile is the beginning of love." Either way, if you are actively looking, or about to start looking for a soulmate, this book will clearly explain to you the ten steps that will compel you to get out of your comfort zone and start searching like a pro. You will be equipped with appropriate information that will lead you to your beloved soulmate in no time. Falling in love is an amazing feeling. You deserve to find and conquer the soulmate of your choice. In order to build a sustainable lifetime relationship, you need to have clarity in your mind. Approach every relationship with your eyes and ears open. Remain alert during your conversations. Follow the ten steps listed in this book, for the greatest adventure of finding the love of your life!